Praise for *The Call*

"Amidst the din of the everyday, we continually respond ~~to the demands~~ of the outer life. David Spangler, on~~ce again, reminds us of~~ ~~the importance~~, our deeper need to reconnect with ~~our inner selves~~ ~~and open a~~ doorway to this realm."

"David Spangler takes a look at the questions that need to be asked."
—*The Atlanta Journal-Constitution*

"What a pleasure to read David Spangler's book."
—Thomas Moore,
author of *Care of the Soul*

"Simple and compelling . . . This book will be useful to anyone wanting help in learning how to listen to and follow his or her inner calling."
—*The New Times* (Seattle)

"What a wonderful book! I recommend it to anyone who has ever been called or wished they'd been called or wondered why they hadn't been called. This book is so wise, yet so simple. A true little gem."
—Ellen Burstyn

"Fresh . . . tender and thoughtful . . . It is an opportune springboard to examining one's direction in life, and to redefining one's purpose and plan."
—*NAPRA ReView*

"David Spangler inspires us to remember that the essence of every 'calling,' no matter how small or large, actually is a summons to love, to be, and to serve. This provocative book relentlessly uncovers, discovers, and recovers the many calls that are present in all aspects of our lives. No one is not called—what an awesome, alluring, and authentic reminder!"
—Angeles Arrien, Ph.D.,
author of *The Four-Fold Way*

"Tightly and beautifully crafted . . . buy the book, and take a very cumbersome load of anxiety off your shoulders."
—*Access*

The Call

A Pilgrim in Aquarius

Everyday Miracles

Revelation: The Birth of a New Age

Emergence: The Rebirth of the Sacred

Reimagination of the World

PARENT *as* MYSTIC

MYSTIC *as* PARENT

David Spangler

RIVERHEAD BOOKS

New York

Riverhead Books
Published by The Berkley Publishing Group
A division of Penguin Putnam Inc.
375 Hudson Street
New York, New York 10014

First Riverhead hardcover edition: January 1999
First Riverhead trade paperback edition: February 2000
Riverhead trade paperback ISBN: 1-57322-778-1

The Penguin Putnam Inc. World Wide Web site address is
http://www.penguinputnam.com

The Library of Congress has catalogued the Riverhead hardcover edition as follows:

Spangler, David.
Parent as mystic, mystic as parent / by David Spangler.
ISBN 1-57322-106-6
1. Parenting—Religious aspects. 2. Mysticism I. Title.
BL625.8.S63 1998   98-36005 CIP
291.4'41—dc21

PRINTED IN THE UNITED STATES OF AMERICA

10 9 8 7 6 5 4 3 2 1

ACKNOWLEDGMENTS

A BOOK EMERGES FROM THE CO-CREATIVE EFFORTS OF many minds and talents. I am always in awe of how people can take my words and, through the excellence of their own skills and their love for what they do, turn them into a final product that is attractive, appealing, and in every way more excellent than it might have been had the whole process been up to me alone. So one of the most pleasurable tasks I have as a writer is to say thank you to these people and to acknowledge their wonderful contributions.

In this instance, this book would not even exist were it

not for my publisher, Susan Petersen, who had the original idea as well as the confidence that I would have something interesting and useful to say on the topic of parenting. Writing this book turned out to be pure fun and gave me the opportunity to reflect more deeply on the inner side of parenting, which cannot help but make me a better parent. So, thank you, Susan! Equally, my editor, Wendy Carlton, has been a joy to work with. Her skill and craft have helped me immeasurably in clarifying my ideas and expressing them well. Besides, her humor made the process of rewriting a delight and not a chore. And on those rare occasions when Wendy wasn't available and I needed help, editorial assistant Jennifer Repo more than filled the bill. Thank you both, Wendy and Jennifer.

As ever, I have nothing but appreciation for the work that my agent, Ned Leavitt, did as well to make this book possible. His encouragement and friendship also gave me the confidence to proceed. Thanks, Ned.

For the beauty of this book, which makes it a pleasure to look at and to read, I want to thank Martha Ramsey, the copy editor; Lisa Ferris in production; and the interior designer, Chris Welch. Thank you each for transforming my work from something ordinary into something beautiful through your own artistry.

Royce Becker is responsible for the beautiful cover and jacket design. Royce produced the cover and sent me a copy while I was still writing the manuscript. When I saw it, I was astonished and thrilled to see that, without his knowing about the book's content, he had captured perfectly in the cover photo one of the key metaphors for parenting that I was using. (Are you telepathic, Royce?) Looking at the photo he chose as I wrote, more than once helped inspire me when I felt stuck. Thank you, Royce, very much.

Finally, in addition to dedicating the book to them, I also want to thank my wife, Julie, and my four wonderful children, John-Michael, Aidan, Kaitlin, and Maryn. Thank you for supporting me in my writing, which can at times keep me from being with you when you would like. Without you I would not be a parent but just a mystic, and a lonely and less wise one at that.

To be a good father, it helps to have great parents and in-laws, to marry someone who is a great wife and mother, and to have kids who are such fine individuals in themselves that they make parenting look easy.

I lucked out with all three.

So this book is dedicated with love and appreciation to the ones who make me look good as a father:

> *Hazel and Marshall and Betty and Roger, our parents;*
> *Julie, my wife;*
> *John-Michael, Aidan, Kaitlin, and Maryn, our children.*

And to parents—and mystics—everywhere.

Contents

Introduction   *1*

MYSTING   *7*

FOSTERING   *17*

INCARNATION   *28*

BIRTH   *35*

CARING   *42*

LAPS   *51*

LISTENING   *58*

Aliens   65

Fields   74

Faith   84

Selfing   98

Images   106

Emergence   115

Bones   123

Ghosts   133

Wounds   144

Time   154

Spirituality   162

Calling   173

Love   178

Edges   181

Suggested Reading   189

PARENT AS MYSTIC
MYSTIC AS PARENT

INTRODUCTION

LET ME BE CLEAR AT THE BEGINNING. THIS IS NOT A how-to book for either parents or mystics. The details of how a parent raises a child depend very much on the personalities involved and the environment and life situations that provide the context. Not knowing those things, I would hesitate to make suggestions. Besides, there are already many fine books available that give excellent advice, instructions, and techniques both for parenting and for the spiritual path. Some of the ones my wife Julie and I have found the most helpful or interesting are listed in the suggested reading section.

What I have sought to do in this book is convey the overall spirit that guides Julie and me in our parenting. Not that you won't find insights or suggestions in the following pages. I hope that you do. But this book is more a personal celebration of the way in which the mystical and parental paths can parallel each other and come together in wonderful ways. It is a celebration of the mystic within the parent and vice versa.

The suggestion for writing this book came from Susan Petersen, my publisher. When Susan first broached the subject of my writing a book on parenting, I was dubious. Having four children, I certainly have experience as a parent, but I have never felt myself to be an expert on the process. I do what comes naturally and what seems right at the time, taking care that whatever I do is mixed with large doses of lovingness, and then I hope for the best! I have great faith in the wisdom and power of the spirit within each of my children, and I figure that my job is divided equally between providing values and direction on the one hand and getting out of the way on the other so that their spirits are free to unfold. I do not see myself as molding my children (or raising them using a set of techniques) as much as I see myself as co-creating their adult futures with them. This approach works for us, but it's not the stuff out of which parenting handbooks are written.

However, once Susan said she didn't want another how-to book either but was looking for something inspirational and empowering to parents, I felt better about the project. For if there is any group of people whom I would like to celebrate, honor, and empower, it is parents. They have the most challenging and important job in the world. I don't think I am indulging in hyperbole to say that the fate of our world rests in the laps of parents. The way we raise our children opens up or closes off possibilities that will shape our future.

As for the mystical side, well, my perspective on life is informed by the spiritual and mystical experiences I have had. It creates the context for how and why I do things as I do; it certainly creates the context for my parenting.

But over the years, I have felt that mysticism is misunderstood. It is often seen as something otherworldly, away from the demands of life, or as a practice or set of techniques separate from the ordinary things we do. But this is not how I experience it at all. Mysticism, to me, describes a way of seeing life, a way of connecting with the world; it is a path of incarnation, not of escape. It is a state of being, rather than a set of techniques.

And it is inclusive, not separative. A nonmystic might think in terms of there being a mystical path and an everyday, worldly path. But a mystic would not see it that way. The heart of the mystical experience is the belief that there is only one path, and it is life itself. Mystics do not make definitions or draw boundaries that say, "Here is where spirituality begins and the mundane ends," or "Over here is the sacred, and over there is everything else."

On the other hand, the mystical does transform the ordinary in wonderful ways, opening it up to broader, deeper realms, like walking out to the edge of a dock jutting out from the shore and discovering yourself surrounded by an ocean of being that you might not have seen before.

Just as parents introduce their children to an increasingly wider experience of the world, so does mysticism guide us out into a broader ocean of life to discover a connectedness and wholeness that otherwise remains invisible. I experience mysticism as a way of living my life in a caring and fostering way. But that is what parents do as well, at least in the context of their children. In many ways, parents are practical mystics.

I felt that by pointing this out, it would inspire parents, celebrating and honoring the challenging role that they play by showing how it connects with a larger dimension of spirituality. And I felt it would also put into perspective just what mysticism is all about, allowing us to see it as an integral part of life and not as a path away from the everyday world.

We may think of mysticism as the dimension of complex issues of theology and spiritual cosmology, but it is really much simpler. It is, at heart, about learning how to recognize and work with the connectedness of the world, the wholeness of all things. Love is at its root, and love is equally at the root of what we do as parents. It is in the spirit of this common rootedness that the parent embodies the mystic and the mystic the parent.

I had mystical experiences most of my life, some coming spontaneously, others unfolding by intent and spiritual practice. However, when I was thirty-eight, Julie and I had our first child. If I thought I understood the mystical path before, it was nothing to what I have learned in the past fifteen years in being a parent to four wonderful individuals: John-Michael, Aidan, Kaitlin, and Maryn.

It may seem strange to equate mysticism with parenting. The one seems so transcendent and pure while the other seems so mundane and—with four kids at least—messy! But mysticism for me is not only giving one's attention to transcendence, for the love and creativity that is at the heart of the sacred is not found only in some higher, numinous realm. It is found all around us, waiting to be recognized and nurtured, and a mystic seeks to find these qualities and the presence from which they emerge, in the places and people that make up our world. A mystic to me is someone who aligns with the transcendental in order to serve and assist the incarnational. A mystic seeks the presence of God not to escape the world but to be more present in the world in a loving and empowering way. And nothing draws you into the world in a loving and empowering way more than learning to be a good parent.

Of all human relationships, surely parenting is one in which we are most called upon to re-create the primal universal dynamics of co-creation and emergence, love and adventure, discovery and delight, caring and compassion. It is the relationship in which we are most expected to embody the presence of the Beloved.

It is a path of resonating with the primal spiritual forces that wrought the universe into being.

It is possible to find that path in some solitary mountain cave or in the midst of a monastery. But I have found it by being a parent.

When I began this book, I had hopes that my wife, Julie, would join me as co-author, for in our family our parenting blends together in seamless ways. Ironically, at the same time she was hired by a local school to develop and teach parent education classes, a project that has demanded much of her time and at which she has excelled. This meant, though, that she was not available to help with the writing.

Consequently, this book is written in my voice, but her spirit is present on every page, for much of what I have learned of parenting I have learned from her and with her. For her help as my partner in raising our family, believe me, I am one thankful mystic.

MYSTING

THREE OTHER MEN AND I HAVE TAKEN THE MORNING OFF
to meet in the local Starbucks to drink mochas and lattés and
reflect on The Meaning of Life. In another time and place,
we might have been tilting our chairs back against a store-
front, our feet up on a porch railing, eating crackers drawn
from a barrel and cheese hacked off from a block sitting on
the store counter, watching the world go by as we pondered

the big questions: What is God? What is Life? Just how long have those crackers been in that barrel? We're partaking in a social ritual. Like monkeys grooming each other, we are plucking tasty ideas out of our mental fur.

This morning the ideas have been wide-ranging, but eventually the conversation has turned to what it means to lead a mystically oriented life. What does it mean to be a mystic? As we roll this question around among us, the usual images arise that one might expect: a mystic is someone who seeks communion with the sacred; a mystic seeks the essence of things; a mystic has a spiritual practice of prayer, meditation, and contemplation. For all their familiarity (more likely because of it), I find these images unsatisfactory and incomplete. They do not convey the richness, the intimacy, or the naturalness of what I experience in my own life; they suggest a path that is too otherworldly, too removed from the bone and blood of everyday life. There is a suggestion of a barrier between the mystic and the ordinary Jane or Joe, a membrane separating the spiritual from the mundane. These familiar images are too redolent of the numinous and the transcendent. Particularly as a parent, I find it hard to relate to them.

Unfortunately, before we can really sink our teeth into this particularly wriggly and lively idea, it is time to go. We all have other appointments and tasks awaiting us, so the resolution of the question will have to wait for another time and another round of mochas. But the question is very useful for me as I return home to continue writing this book. For in looking at the ways in which a parent is like a mystic, and vice versa, as a means of illuminating deeper aspects of both the mystical and the parental life, the question of what a mystic is and what a mystic does—what it is that makes a person a mystic—is very pertinent indeed.

The word itself does not give us any obvious clues. A writer writes. A plumber plumbs. A teacher teaches. A mystic mysts? That sounds like a computer game or someone who moonlights as a water sprinkler.

However, *mystic* and *mystery* both come from the same Greek root, *myst,* which refers to initiation into the "mysteries," the secret teachings about the nature of humankind and the world that lay at the heart of Greek religion. In this sense, a mystic is someone who seeks deeper knowledge about reality, someone who seeks the essence of wisdom and truth. From there it is not too great a jump to the most common definition of a mystic as someone who seeks communion and oneness with God, who, after all, is the source, the truth, and the essence of all things.

How one does this seeking, however, depends on how one defines God, communion, truth, and essence. In the history of such things, mystics have pursued their inner craft in as wide a variety of ways as people do in any other occupation. Some have been hermits and recluses, living away from the distractions of everyday life, while others have been householders and parents. Some have been quiet contemplatives; others have been teachers, social and political activists, and administrators. Some have been pacifists; others have been warriors. Some have sought escape from the earth; others have embraced the world, seeing it as the body of the Beloved. Some have sought union with God through prayer and devotion; others have done so through study, relationships, sports, work, and service.

To further complicate the issue, the word *mystic* is also applied to any person who engages in activities that involve the metaphysical. A recent book, for example, *The Executive Mystic,* essentially offers techniques for developing one's intuitive and psychic skills and offers simple, benign magical rituals to enhance one's competitive edge. But nowhere in the book will a reader find any mention of God, communion, prayer, contemplation, the surrender of the ego, or the transcending of personal desires in seeking oneness with the sacred—all of which are part of the classical mystical tradition.

So, although one person may portray mysticism as a set of down-to-earth, practical power tools for getting the job done and succeeding in business, for others anything mystical smacks of obfuscation, superstition, otherworldliness, and unrealistic, irresponsible, head-in-the-clouds thinking (or not-thinking, as the case may be). A Protestant minister once took me aside at a conference to offer me some friendly advice, which was that I should not call myself a mystic because it did me an injustice. "David, you are too levelheaded and practical to be tarnished with the image of mysticism," he told me. "It will give people the wrong impression of you!" I appreciated his kindness and concern, but as you can see, I have yet to take his advice.

If, then, a mystic can be variously seen in our culture as a religious contemplative locked away in a cloister somewhere; a powerful, magical executive succeeding at business through the strength of her psychic abilities; or a misguided, otherworldly oaf, where does that leave someone like me, who doesn't fit into any of these images and whose response when someone asks me what I do is to say, "I am a father"?

What do I do, personally, that justifies the claim of being a mystic?

Do I seek oneness with the sacred? Yes, but I seek a blending and engagement with the world as well, since for me the presence of the sacred is everywhere. Do I honor the spiritual side of life? Yes, but I also honor the bone and blood, the dirt and grass. Life is an energy that reaches from the heavens to the earth and from the bottoms of my feet to the top of my soul, as well as outward into the world. Why favor part of it and ignore the rest? I give equal weight to the sparkling energies of spirit and the juicy greenness of life. Do I spend my life in retreat and contemplation, prayer and silence? With four kids? Hardly! Yet I do take time every day for a quick attunement to listen to my inner self and its connections with a larger universe and to be aware of the sacred in that moment. Do I seek wisdom? As a father, you bet! I can use all the wisdom I can get. (And as for initiation into the mysteries of humankind, I would love to understand what goes on in my kids' minds sometimes!)

In short, while I have my still times of silence and meditation, mostly I practice a running mysticism in which I search for the loving silence and the energy of delight and compassion in the midst of fixing lunches, carpooling, helping with homework, washing dishes, and playing games.

Of course, this is what most parents do. The mystical trick is to see all these activities as woven into a larger whole, like a quilt where each square is separate but all are connected into something that is warm and embracing. What a mystic does is connect. He or she is a bridge between worlds, the point of contact where spirit and matter meet in an eruption of joy and co-creativity or in a depth of insight and understanding. A mystic is the membrane between the worlds of the sacred and the mundane, respecting both sides and allowing love and nourishment to flow between them in mutually beneficial ways.

A mystic turns fragments into wholenesses, pieces into patterns, and connects these with the great underlying wholeness or pattern that I call the Beloved. And the tools for doing this are attitudes of attentiveness, compassion, respect, and delight—tools with which parents are very familiar.

A mystic re-members.

It is easy in the midst of an average day to begin doing one's tasks in an automatic, half-awake manner, to allow each event to remain unconnected to any larger wholeness. Our kids go to three different schools, and we carpool to each of them on different days. I have been embarrassed more than once to discover that I have inadvertently started taking one group of kids to the wrong school because I have acted out of habit from the day before. I became dis-connected, something that happens all too easily in our fast paced culture. I forgot I was a mystic!

Seeing and remembering the patterns and wholenesses of one's life is just a step away from expanding that vision to see and remember the connection one has with the larger wholeness of the sacred, the larger pattern of all life. And when one remembers that larger vision, everything falls into perspective. In the midst of activity, one relaxes, and when one relaxes, love and energy begin to flow naturally.

The traditional definition of a mystic is one who seeks communion with God. But for me, that communion is only the first step. For that communion, in my experience, is not the loss of self but the filling of self to overflowing. One becomes a cup running over with love and delight, a cup that others can share.

The sharing is the essential mystical act for me. That is what a mystic does in the midst of life, just as a writer writes or a plumber plumbs. A mystic brings the love and delight, creativity and compassion, respect and connection to the activities, places, and people around her, allowing these impulses to flow from the strength and clarity of her own inner connection. This flow can be a strong, transformative, healing burst of energy if need be, but more often it is a sense of peace, calm, and loving presence filling a situation like a gentle mist.

(Which, I guess, lets me say that a mystic really does myst.)

Is it this easy to do? About as easy as parenting. Which is to say, not at all, and yes. Parenting is the most challenging, demanding, exasperating, frightening, rewarding, enchanting, consuming, exciting job I can think of. It almost always calls you to your edge and then asks you to go beyond it, in the same way that God calls a mystic to the edge, and then beyond. Parenting and mysticism both are hard on little selves that want their own way; both demand that we mature. Both demand time and attention. Both demand learning and changing and growing, not always our favorite occupations.

Yet, when each of my children was born, I was filled with a love that made me believe I could overcome any obstacle that presented itself. And over the years, in the presence of that love, I have found parenting, for all its challenge and work, still curiously effortless—or perhaps, like a runner, who enters "the Zone," I discover a flow in my parenting that sustains me and makes it seem easy. There is a naturalness, even simplicity, about it that gives me momentum. That naturalness is grounded in such simple actions as paying attention, being available, sharing delight, listening, respecting, loving, participating.

The same has been true for my mystical practice. There is a tendency in our culture to see connecting with the sacred as the gold medal at the end of the spiritual Olympics, a feat of astonishing inner athleticism. In fact, the same simple acts open us to that connection: paying attention, being open and available, sharing delight, and participating in life. The sacred is not in some galaxy far, far away or at the end of a long, exhausting life of religious and metaphysical exercises. It is as close as that which brings us delight and a sense of well-being and love; it is as close as that which opens us up to new understanding and insight, even if that opening may be temporarily painful; it is as close as that which touches us with life and gives us vitality. It is as close as a blue sky, a lover's smile, a child's laughter, a challenging task, another's need.

A child comes naturally to us, born out of an act of great pleasure, intimacy, and love. God comes to us similarly in the intimacy, the pleasure inherent in life. Making the child and making the connection with God is simple when we open to what comes naturally.

What is challenging is what comes after—the deepening of the relationship and the fulfilling of the responsibilities it brings, along with the opportunities for growth and change and co-creativity. This is true for any relationship, whether between a husband and wife, a parent and child, or a soul and the Beloved.

Fulfilling those relationships is what being a parent and a mystic is all about, but whether we are parenting or mysting, they are both rooted in love.

FOSTERING

A FEW MONTHS AFTER OUR FIRST CHILD, JOHN-MICHAEL, was born, Julie and I drove down from Madison, Wisconsin, to show him off to my parents, who live in Dayton, Ohio. En route, we stopped for lunch at a Bob Evans restaurant along the Interstate. All went well until near the end of our meal when Julie announced she needed to change the baby's diaper. Feeling that this was a good occasion to gain daddy points, I said, "Oh, no, you finish your lunch. I'll do it!" Off I went to the men's restroom with John-Michael in one arm and the diaper bag in the other. How innocuous and seemingly innocent those first steps into Hell can be.

As the enlightened nineties were still a decade away, the architect for this men's room had obviously been guided by two ancient principles: men do not change diapers, and men do not need much room to go to the bathroom. The narrow room was barely wide enough for a toilet stall and a sink with minimal counter space. Where to put John-Michael while I did the deed? Where to put the diaper bag? Where, in fact, to put myself?

Feeling an ominously large squishiness underneath his pants, I laid my son down on the edge of the sink counter while I tried to maneuver the diaper bag off my shoulder. It had a large flap of cloth on one side that could be folded out into a makeshift changing pad, and I decided to spread it all out on the floor. However, the countertop was cold and damp, which started Johnny crying and thrashing about. One little foot went flying out, hit the diaper bag, and knocked it upside down into a garbage bin near the sink. I could hear all the stuff inside it falling out with a clatter into the darkness of the trash. To make matters worse, the more Johnny flailed about, the more a stain spread around his pants as the contents of his diaper began to ooze out.

What to do? I couldn't leave Johnny perched precariously on the counter, and I didn't want to just plop him onto the floor while I rummaged through the garbage for the contents of the diaper bag. So I gingerly held him upright with one hand while I reached in the garbage with the other and pulled out the bag, which had gotten stuck. I was finally able to get the bag onto the floor, and Johnny onto the cloth, but by now he was in full tantrum mode. The problem now was that the fresh diapers and all the cleaning wipes were still somewhere in the bottom of the garbage can.

I won't go into all the details of the next few minutes, except that to say "The shit hit the fan" doesn't begin to convey what it does when in the presence of a flailing, crying baby. At one point, no doubt attracted by the screams and cries coming from the restroom, the manager looked in to find out what was going on, turned pale, and quickly closed the door.

Finally, I had John-Michael newly diapered. And at this point, desperate that no unsuspecting male would feel the call of nature and walk into the disaster area that had once been a restroom, I grabbed Johnny, ran out to where Julie was sitting, and practically threw him at her. "Here!" I blurted. "I've got to go back and clean up." With every pair of eyes in the place fixed on me, I ran back into the restroom, locked the door, and began the process of cleaning my own version of the Augean stables, as well as rescuing the remaining contents of the diaper bag from the garbage.

Knowing how to gracefully change a diaper on a kicking and squirming infant without liberally distributing its contents all over oneself, the child, and the environment is a vital parental skill, usually learned sooner rather than later (and preferably not through on-the-job training in a roadside restaurant). There are many skills that parents learn that are specific to their role as child-bearers and child-rearers. But one of the most important, if not the most important, is a skill that goes far beyond the boundaries of parenting and links the task of a parent with that of a mystic.

That skill is fostering.

I have a friend who grew up in several state-supported foster homes, shuttled from one to another as circumstances beyond his control would change. Though he was never badly mistreated or abused in any of these homes, he never experienced much in the way of consistent and heartfelt caring. As he once put it to me, "I was pretty much left on my own to raise myself as best I could." In effect, he became his own parent. That he turned out to be an empathetic and caring man is a testament to his own innate spiritual strength.

I have another friend who is a foster parent with several children under her and her husband's care. She gives wholly of herself and is full of embracing love for each of the children who live in her home. Like many other foster parents, she performs a difficult job with grace and skill, setting a standard that any parent would be proud to live up to.

Still, in spite of the excellent example that she and other foster parents like her provide, the image of foster parenting in our society seems to be shaped more by the kind of situations my first friend experienced, if not worse. Foster parenting is often regarded as a kind of substitute parenting, inadequate when compared to the real thing.

The heart of parenting, however, lies precisely in the skill of fostering. For to foster is to raise up into actuality what otherwise would remain as potential. It means, according to my *Random House* dictionary, "to care for and cherish, to promote development and growth, to encourage and to rear." As a mystic might say (and this one does), what could be more essential and basic than that to parenting?

There are many ways to be considered a parent. I can be called a parent simply for having contributed my genetic material to the creation of a child, for having biologically sired a daughter or son. I can be called a parent for legal reasons as well, as when I adopt or take on legal guardianship of a child who is not my own offspring. I can become a stepparent by marrying someone else who has children.

As news stories tell us with depressing regularity, being a biological or legal parent is no guarantee that I will "care for and cherish, promote the development and growth of, or encourage and rear" a child. Assuming I do not abandon my child and not parent at all, I may instead abuse and manipulate, harm and neglect, stunt and distort the life and growth of my child. I may, with the authority of being a biological or legal parent, act as an antiparent. Sometimes, qualifying as the noun "parent" has little to do with whether a person fulfills the spirit of the verb "parenting."

If I am a true parent, however my parentship has come about, then I am a fostering parent. At the very least, parenthood means to be one who fosters. It may also mean that I am genetically linked to my children, or that I legally have the authority and responsibility for their welfare, their upbringing, and their relationship to society for a certain term of years. But biology, authority, and responsibility only augment my fostering; they do not replace it, nor are they in themselves proper substitutes for it.

To foster is to care for a life, to nourish it, and to bring forth its potentials. This can apply to more than just raising a child. I may foster a plan, a project, an ideal, or a goal. A mentor may foster someone's career, a doctor may foster someone's health. Right now, I am fostering this book, while in my classes, I seek to foster peoples' exploration and development of their own spirituality.

To foster is to be aware of and supportively responsive to the emergence of an interior life with its particular energy and possibilities. This is what every good parent seeks to do for his or her children; to create conditions that allow a child to unfold and enter the world in the best possible way. This is precisely what a mystic is called to do as well: to be aware of, and to support, a spirit and sacredness within the world that, like the potentials of a child, is seeking to emerge.

A cosmologist might say that within the universe is an impulse toward self-organization, emergence, and increasing complexity. A biologist might say that within life is an impulse toward growth and evolution. A psychologist might say that within each of us are possibilities that can be nourished and given expression. There is a common intuition, a sense that there is something within us and within the world that seeks to grow and unfold, to make a new contribution to the ongoing emergence of creation. A mystic takes this intuition seriously and acts accordingly. And the primary nature of that action is fostering.

Fostering is a spirit of honoring the emerging life, potential, or soul. It is a spirit of caring. It is a spirit of love. It is a spirit of wisdom, for as each person and thing in creation is unique, so must my fostering be tailored to that uniqueness. Consequently, it is also a spirit of listening and paying attention.

For example, one evening we all were watching an episode of *America's Funniest Home Videos* on television, in which a succession of strangers fell off horses, slipped on dance floors, had walls fall on them, and generally endured various hilarious moments of humiliation and pain. In response to this candid series of disasters and slapstick events that would have left the Three Stooges green with envy, Julie, John-Michael, Aidan, and I were shrieking with merriment in true Seinfeldian disregard for the possible suffering involved when I realized that my oldest daughter, Kaitlin, wasn't laughing. When I stopped chortling enough to ask her why, she said, "But Daddy, there's nothing funny here. These people are getting hurt!"

Now, insensitive clod that I am, this insightful pronouncement from my five-year-old daughter did not stop me from watching and enjoying this television show (what can I say?—I was raised on Buster Keaton and the Bowery Boys). But it did make me realize that her sense of humor was quite different from my own and from everyone else's in the family (and equally delightful in its own way). I am a playful teaser, usually with puns and wordplay but in other ways as well, but as a young child, Kaitlin always wanted me to be straight with her and not "joke her," as she put it. So in fostering her as a unique individual and an equal member of the family, I have had to learn different styles of relating. To do that successfully, I have had to curb my automatic ways of behaving, to listen, and to be mindful of just what each of my children needs from me in order to feel honored and in good communication.

Fostering is one way—perhaps the main way—that we enter into a co-creative relationship with the world around us. It is how we engage in partnership with the sacred. For God is to me the ultimate foster parent, inviting us to express our own sacredness by participating in the cherishing and nurturing of creation. To put it another way, spiritually and practically, we are instruments of the Divine in fostering the world.

This may sound impressive, but, in practice, it is very ordinary. To be a good mystic, it is useful to think like a parent. For a parent can have a vision of a child's possibilities and see the Divine in that child, but when it comes time to change the diapers or prepare a meal, philosophy must give way to practical action in the moment. Parents know that the fulfillment of their vision for their child unfolds in the myriad ordinary details of everyday life.

The art of parenting—of fostering—is made up of hundreds of little moments of being accessible, of paying attention, of making a lap, of playing games, of opening arms for hugs, of instilling discipline and honor, of cooking meals, of washing clothes, and of changing diapers. Fostering is wiping noses and holding sick children while they throw up; it is singing to them as they go to bed, telling them stories, making sure they brush their teeth, putting them into pajamas. It is attending school plays and meetings with teachers, sports events, and field trips. It is driving carpool. It is making sure they have good values—values that respect and empower others as well as themselves—and can stick to them. And in the midst of doing all these things and more, it is remaining aware of the larger vision.

In short, fostering is made up of ordinary activities undertaken in the spirit of an underlying love and determination to do whatever is necessary to enable your child to enter the world as a healthy, productive, creative, imaginative, joyous, responsible, and capable human being. Likewise, spiritual practice is largely made up of ordinary activities undertaken in a spirit of bringing forth the presence of the sacred in as healthy, creative, joyous, clear, and integrated a manner as possible.

To be a mystic is in many ways to be a parent, without the biological or legal connection to that which one is fostering. But a mystic knows that there are deeper bonds of communion and shared life that transcend biology, law, and society, and it is these bonds that inform his or her fostering spirit. A mystic is one who fosters the shared soul and life of the world.

For a parent, that shared life manifests in very particular ways as specific children. A parent is like a mystic dedicated to fostering the unfolding of the world through the instrument of a family. Like a mystic, a parent must attune to what is not yet visible, to what is seeking to emerge, in order to weave that spirit into the flesh and bone and behavior of children who as adults will delight in and contribute to the world at large.

The challenge of human life is to build a bridge over which the infinite and the universal may connect with the finite and the particular, allowing the potentials of the former to blend with the energy of the latter in ways that benefit and uplift the whole of life.

Fostering, as a characteristic of both mystic and parent, is the art of building that bridge.

INCARNATION

ONE OF THE THINGS FOR WHICH SEATTLE IS FAMOUS, other than lattés and rain, is the Space Needle. Looking for all the world like a flying saucer perched on top of a tripod, it was built for the 1962 World's Fair. Six hundred and five feet at its tallest point, with a revolving restaurant on top, it no longer dominates the Seattle skyline, having been eclipsed years ago by even taller sykscrapers downtown. But its gracefulness and distinct appearance still catch and captivate the eye. When friends come to visit, it is often one of the local landmarks they want to see.

However, the Space Needle is only one attraction at the Seattle Center, and the real fun of visiting there, for me, is the Science Museum and the IMAX theater. It was there in the gift shop that I spotted (and to my regret, did not purchase, since I have not seen it since) a poster that summed up a certain spiritual perspective. It was a poster of our galaxy, the Milky Way. One arrow pointed toward the earth, way out on the edge of one of the spiral arms, and said, "You Are Here!" Another arrow pointed to the center of the galaxy, ablaze with the light of a million stars, and said, "All the Good Stuff Is Here!"

This poster humorously captures the transcendentalist perspective that all the "good stuff" we long for, the home we seek, the peace and fulfillment we desire, is not to be found here on earth but somewhere else: in Heaven, in the spirit realms, in transcendental states of oneness, anywhere but in the midst of matter. Earth, on the other hand, is the "vale of tears," the place of exile, of illusion and dreams, the place from which to be rescued, the place of sin and evil and all that is not of the spirit. It is not our true home.

In contrast is the recent movie *Michael,* with John Travolta as the archangel Michael. Michael is no transcendental, airy-fairy, translucent being. He is a muscular, hairy, smoking, beer-drinking, sugar-eating winged angel who loves battles and women. He is masculinity and power incarnate. But he believes in the power of little miracles to effect great change, and he takes delight in the unusual and quirky things that humans create (such as the world's largest ball of twine or the world's largest nonstick frying pan). He simply loves the earth for all that it is—for its soil, its clouds, its vibrant and diverse life—and he treasures the limited time he can spend here. Michael is an incarnationalist.

I suppose there is a popular image of mystics as transcendentalists, and I have certainly known people who set out on a mystical path because they found everyday life in the world difficult and unattractive. But that has not been my experience. When I am in my deepest communion with spirit, that is when I experience my closest connection with the earth. Conversely, often when I am engaged in the most ordinary activities, I experience a sense of mystical unity and energy. Like Michael, my spirit is called and uplifted by the vitality and music of the world. I find the Beloved as much in the concrete things around me as in transcendental states of consciousness.

So, for me, the mystical path is a path of incarnation. It is a path of enjoying and delighting in the world, a path of putting flesh on the potentials of spirit, giving them form and particularity. A mystic is someone who sees the transcendental nature of incarnation (or the incarnational potential of the transcendent) and brings these two polarities together in appropriate ways.

Which is why the parental and the mystical paths seem to me to go hand in hand, for a parent is by definition an instrument of incarnation, the portal through which a human soul becomes part of the world. And making love may be transcendental, but once a child is conceived, it is incarnation all the way.

From the very beginning, a parent's tasks are intimately connected to a child's body. We feed, clean, cuddle, rub, protect, and cherish these instruments of incarnation. Nothing in the world is quite as satisfying, quite as sensual and heartful, as feeling a baby's tiny body snuggle close to yours. We rejoice when they turn over, we get excited when they crawl, we haul out cameras and video recorders to immortalize their first steps. We make marks on doors or walls to measure their growth. I remember my anticipation well, waiting for each of my children to say their first words and, when they did, greeting them with joy as if they had been pronouncements from heaven. (Now, of course, I have forgotten what they said—though I'm sure it must have been "Daddy"—except for Aidan. His first word was "meat." He's been the family carnivore ever since.)

A friend of mine owns a toy store (and thereby ranks in my estimation, and that of my kids, as only a little lower than an archangel). Julie and I went in there the other day to find a birthday present and were greeted by our friend, bubbling over the fact that his newborn son had laughed for the first time that morning. "I was a half-hour late getting to work by the time I had all the recorders set up to capture the moment," he laughed, his eyes beaming with joy that would make any mystic envious. What a trip parenting can be!

If we delight in our children's growth and change, we are equally thrilled by introducing the world to them. "Look!" I exclaim to my youngest daughter, Maryn, with an excitement worthy of seeing Jean-Luc Picard, captain of the starship *Enterprise,* coming up the walk to my front door. "There's a doggie on the front lawn!" And "There's a tree! And a bird! And those are clouds!" Or "Taste this! See, it's green like a little tree. You'll be like a giant eating a little tree! What fun! It's called broccoli . . ." And remember the kick of introducing your children to chocolate? (Or, in our case, the older children introducing the younger ones months before we would have: "I know you don't have teeth yet, Kaitlin, but suck on this. It's a Hershey bar!")

There is nothing abstract or transcendental about any of these things, though they can certainly be points of connection with the transcendent. We celebrate the physicality of our children and their interaction with the earth. We celebrate first steps, first teeth, first sounds. We celebrate their seeing, their hearing, their tasting, their smelling, their touching. And we celebrate the things they see, hear, taste, smell, and touch.

We work to make our children citizens of the green and juicy earth. My deepest wish as a father is that my children will grow to be creative, responsible, and loving partners with their world, able to contribute in their own unique ways. I want them to feel at home here, to know that there is good stuff on their earth as well as at the center of the galaxy, to realize that we live in a world that still has mysteries and wonders to explore; one that may be dangerous and dark in parts but still a friendly and welcoming place. I want them to rejoice in their incarnations, and in the singular, specific character of their lives as doorways through which the infinite can enter and bless the world.

In the down-and-dirty connection with earthly things that all parents must have, and in the celebration of that connection that most parents feel as they nourish and watch the growth of their children, there is a powerful model for what it means to be a mystic. If mysticism were a profession like medicine, and mystics had to take an oath before they could practice, I fantasize that it would go like this: "As a mystic I vow to uphold the importance and glory of incarnation, seeing it not as a separation from God but as an ongoing, ever-emerging fulfillment of God's desire for self-expression. I vow to honor and take delight in the earth and embrace it as my home and my sustenance. I also vow to honor and take delight in my humanity, with compassion for its challenges and struggles, with rejoicing for its triumphs, and with respect for its potentials. I vow to support all incarnate beings in their innate desire to unfold the highest and most fulfilling that is within them, and I will be a bridge across which the incarnate and the transcendent may meet and blend in co-creative wonder."

I believe parents already have that unspoken vow engraved in their hearts. It comes with the territory.

BIRTH

AS THE DUE DATE FOR OUR FIRST CHILD, JOHN-MICHAEL, approached, Julie and I were ready. Though we would have preferred a home birth, this was difficult to arrange in Wisconsin at that time. So we opted for a birthing room at the local hospital that was set up to resemble a room in a home as much as possible. I had planned out our route to the hospital and had driven it a few times to time myself. To satisfy my new-father paranoia, I even planned out alternate routes in case traffic was heavy. As we got closer to the day, we had an overnight bag ready to go at a moment's notice, and Julie's mom had arrived prepared to lend a hand. As far as I could tell, all systems were go. We were ready!

The only problem was that John-Michael wasn't.

As the due date came and went, we entered a curious time. The doctor said that the baby could come any day; all we could do was wait. And wait. And wait some more.

For the next ten days, it was as if we had stepped out of normal reality and into a timeless domain where not only Julie but also each moment was pregnant with anticipation. Yet it was also a time that was very calm and peaceful. Since we couldn't go far from the house, we felt cocooned and embraced. We knew we had done all we could do, so we had to just sit back and let nature take its course.

Each day, it seemed to me that I went deeper into this state of relaxed anticipation. I was working as a freelance boardgame designer at the time for TSR, the Dungeons and Dragons company. Each day I would take out the game-in-process, testing it, changing it, working on rules. Then I would take walks with Julie and her mom, Betty. I would watch television or listen to music. I would read. Sometimes we would all just sit and talk. Underneath all this normal and ordinary activity there was a current of heightened awareness and expectation. I felt like I was at an edge, and on the other side was a whole new world. I felt as if I were in a womb of sorts, just like John-Michael. I was in the midst of an energy of birthing, poised between the potential and the actual. While this might sound stressful, this boundary place was simultaneously very peaceful and energetic. Amazingly, it was one of the most tranquil times of my life. I loved it!

Then the moment came. Julie and her mom had taken a long walk, and not long after she returned home, labor began. Even then, as we timed the contractions to make sure this was no false alarm, and dashed for the car (and followed my carefully timed route), the peace continued to flow with us and around us. And later that evening, when John-Michael appeared, he pulled me with him down through the birth canal, and into a whole new life.

That moment marked the beginning of my life as a father, but it also marked the beginning of a whole new understanding for me in my mystical practice. To my inner perceptions, the whole of creation is constantly in a state of birthing—myriad possibilities, potentials, insights, energies, and qualities are emerging daily—and we are deeply woven into that process as midwives, participants, creations, creatures, and co-creators all rolled into one.

This understanding has always been one of my essential mystical insights, one of the foundations of my inner practice and belief. But until that week when we waited for John-Michael to stir from the womb, and until the moment he emerged and I cut his umbilical cord and handed him to Julie, I had not felt the reality of that vision in my own blood and bones. It had been an idea for me, a vision, but it had not lived in my cells until I actually participated in giving birth to another life.

Looking back, I remember that experience building up for nine months (and ten days). When Julie became pregnant, it was as if both of us were carrying our new child. In the kind of physical empathy that many fathers experience, I shared many of Julie's physical discomforts during the pregnancy and felt deeply involved in the process. Yet, while Julie was the physical womb, I felt that I also carried the soul of our baby in my own energy, co-creating with Julie an invisible womb of spirit that joined with the physical one to nurture our developing son. This was equally true during each of our later three pregnancies; it never felt to me as if I were just an observer or bystander.

Once John-Michael was born, I got caught up in the novelty of being a new parent. On some days, I felt as if I had slipped into a Disney cartoon where impossibly colorful birds are always landing and twittering gaily on your shoulder and all the trees and flowers sing to you as you pass. It was definitely zip-a-dee-do-dah time. But then, not having learned that as a new parent you *never* wake up unless you have to, hoarding every moment of sleep you can get, I would lie awake at night, the bluebirds gone and the thought of the next twenty years of fatherhood looming above me like the sheerest cliffs of Everest. How was I going to enable this little baby to become a responsible, caring, successful man? Where was the instruction book? Couldn't he just slip back into the womb for another few months while I got better prepared? Surely Julie wouldn't mind . . .

Then John-Michael would wake up and do something cute and babyish, and the bluebirds would be back on my shoulder, my fears dissipating like dew on a summer morning. Over the weeks following his birth, these mood swings smoothed out in the routines of everyday life. Julie and I got on with life and with learning to be parents, and John-Michael settled into the traditional role of the first-born: guinea pig.

One of the basic teachings in many spiritual and mystical traditions is to learn to see the world with fresh eyes every day, to practice what in Zen is called beginner's mind. In Christian scripture, God says, "Behold, I make all things new," and in my mind the practice of a mystic is to recognize that this is not just poetry but reality. In each moment there is a grace that allows us to step sideways out of the linearity of time with its divisions of past, present, and future. It allows us to enter a timelessness in which more is possible than just what the immediate past might suggest or dictate. In this grace, we can see that the moment we are in, and the next moment we will be in, is emerging from the newness of the sacred as well as from the culmination of all that has gone before. While history may dictate, "The next moment must be this way, it must follow the pattern I have set up," the sacred maintains, "The next moment can take many forms; it can follow the logic of the past, or something new can be born that is unexpected and unpredicted, and the world will change accordingly."

The practice of beginner's mind enables us to expand each moment to the possibility of more emerging or more being possible than what we might expect from past experience. It opens possibilities of learning, growth, and surprise. And here is an interesting image: in many of the creation myths of native peoples around the world, the one who creates the world, who brings light, knowledge, and goodness to humanity is often the Trickster god or goddess. It is the god or goddess whose actions cannot be predicted, who operates outside of logic and expectation, and who acts with humor and a sense of the unexpected.

In short, the Trickster acts like children who regularly defy our expectations and who say and do things that make us see the world in a new light and bring freshness to even the most familiar things. Children naturally have beginner's mind; how could it be otherwise? They are seeing the world for the first time. I remember one bright summer day when Aidan was two years old and saw his shadow, realizing for the first time that it was actually a part of him. For several minutes he danced delightedly with his shadow around the yard, watching how it mimicked his every move, laughing with pleasure at this wondrous discovery. It was a magical moment.

That parents can have many such magical moments with their children is why I think we parents have an advantage in the pursuit of mystical insights, for we live all the time with those who embody the sense of birthing, delight, and creative discovery. They invite us to share their perceptions, even as they need our familiarity and understanding of the world. Parent and child can be like past and future, coming together to illumine the present in exciting ways.

Jesus suggested that unless we become like children, we cannot see the kingdom of Heaven around us. It was not childishness to which he was referring, but that inner vision that sees the world free from the tyranny of the familiar, as a place of infinite possibilities always ready to spring newly into being. Sometimes in the midst of our everyday lives, we forget that those possibilities are there. Many things can remind us, but children are especially potent in this regard.

CARING

THE IMAGE OF GOD THAT IS MOST PREVALENT IN JUDEO-Christian religious culture is that of a father. Recent efforts to diminish sexism in theology have been broadening that conception. But even when we think of the feminine side of the sacred, of God as mother or even as Goddess, we are still thinking of a parent. It is more rare to think of God as a child, though that concept does exist in other spiritual traditions. It would be an unusual congregation indeed that would pray on a Sunday morning, "Our Child, Who art in Heaven."

For good reason, of course. Parents create life and give birth to new beings, so it is not strange that the ultimate source of life, the birther of worlds and universes, would be imagined as the ultimate parent. Also parents are seen as the powerful, independent authority figures in our lives, while babies and children are seen as vulnerable and dependent. Who wants to think of God as vulnerable and dependent?

In my own inner experience, the deeper one goes into the presence of the sacred, the more one enters into a mystery that is beyond the imagination, beyond images like "parent," "father," "mother," "child." Yet, early on in my career as a freelance mystic, I began to experience an aspect of the sacred that resonated much more clearly with the image of child than with the image of parent. Whereas the idea of God as a parent would evoke childlike, dependent responses in me, the idea of God as child called to depths of caring and love within me and drew forth my identity as a nourisher. In effect, it called to me to see myself as a parent to the emerging world around me.

For many years I have played in my classes and lectures with images of God and spirit to encourage people to think and look more deeply at the realities behind these images. I have learned that how we think of the sacred, and of the spiritual realm in general, influences how we think of ourselves (and vice versa). For example, if I think of spirit in a hierarchical manner, then I will most likely think of God at the top of the pyramid and me at the bottom. That image can easily lead to feelings of separation and distance between us. (The "all-the-good-stuff-is-elsewhere" idea.) On the other hand, if I think of spirit in a holistic manner as a continuum or an interweaving pattern that has no up or down, higher or lower, then that separation and distance is eliminated; I have a sense of being a valued and loved participant. My caring and compassion can radiate in all directions, unimpeded by hierarchical considerations.

Hierarchies are important as ways of clarifying lines of authority and responsibility, but love itself is not hierarchical. The heart transcends such organizational details. The fact that in a family some of us are parents and some of us are children does not mean that we cannot all be caring and compassionate toward each other. One evening I was going through my monthly routine of paying the bills, wondering, like millions of other fathers, I'm sure, just how to make the budget stretch a bit further that month. I was sitting on the floor with my back against a chair. John-Michael, observing that I was experiencing some stress, came over, sat in the chair behind me, laid his head down on mine, and whispered in my ear, "I love you, Dad." Then he gave me a hug. It didn't add any more money to the bank, but it sure gave my inner economy a huge boost! Similarly, there was a day when I wasn't feeling well, and Maryn came over to rub my back. "You are my baby," she told me. "I am going to make you better." Not long after, Kaitlin appeared with tea and toast for me.

Caring exists in a nonhierarchical dimension. It does not take measure of our power or status, or judge whether we are higher or lower, stronger or weaker, perfect or imperfect. It is not a transaction but a gift between equals. Both parents and mystics are custodians and teachers of this gift. Both seek to nurture the ability to give and receive caring and to understand the nonhierarchical relationship in which it manifests, which is at the heart of a family, as well as at the heart of the world. Many hierarchies fill our world—establishing who is in charge, who has control, how the pecking order is arranged—and the desire is strong to use hierarchies to establish and express one's identity, one's position, and one's power. For this reason, recognizing and enhancing the nonhierarchical dimensions in which we are partners—co-creators—in bringing love and compassion into the world is both important and challenging.

In this context, one of the exercises I give people in my classes is to imagine the sacred as a baby that has been placed into their hands, into their care. What feelings does this evoke? Can these students feel protective of the sacred, can they feel nurturing and caring? Can they feel themselves responsible for the emergence and growth of the sacred in our world?

What I want in this exercise is to confront the feeling that we are children who need to be taken care of, and that if we are good, God will supply all our needs. What I want is for people to experience a very adult sense of responsibility and sense of their power to nourish the blessings of the sacred in their lives and the lives of others. I want them to be participants, not just recipients, in the miracles and mystery of sacredness. I want them to discover that to care is a very mystical thing to do, for caring connects us with the world. When we understand the mystical vision of the world as a new life endlessly unfolding, with each new step beginning in a vulnerable way, then caring becomes a way of nurturing that emergence.

This image has been useful over the years in encouraging people to think more deeply about what the sacred is for them in their lives (and what they are in the life of the sacred). However, it was not until I held our first baby in my arms that I fully experienced right down into my cells just what it meant to be responsible for a life in all its vulnerability and need. The sacred really did become a child for me in the personhood of each of my children, and this evoked in me an experience of caring, responsibility, and nourishing that I had not previously known in such a human and fleshy way. In discovering myself as a father, I discovered more clearly and personally what my mystical practice had been telling me all along.

Can I think of myself as being responsible for and nurturing God rather than the other way around? Considering the difference between myself as a very finite creature and the sacred as the infinite life and essence within all things, the idea might seem laughable and more than a little arrogant. On the other hand, if I don't only think of God in such a large scale—only as "ultimate," "universal," and "BIG"—if I think of God as a seed, as that tiny potential of sacredness, that small moment of love and grace, that fragile instinct toward holiness and wholeness in any situation, then my perspective shifts. For if God is in each moment or can emerge from each moment as a presence of blessing, then we all know just how fragile and vulnerable that emergence can be. It can easily be—and all too often is—overwhelmed by feelings of anger, hatred, fear, desire, fatigue, boredom, and just plain inattentiveness and selfishness.

God is spoken of as a "still, small voice," not as a boombox sitting on our shoulders blaring out instructions, encouragement, guidance, and philosophy. The emphasis in spiritual training is on learning how to listen deeply and not miss that small voice in the midst of the many louder voices and stimulations in human society. This requires caring.

As a parent, I have certainly experienced the ways in which I can squash the emergence of connectedness in a moment. Kaitlin had a hard time learning to ride a bicycle; I don't think her heart was in it. Even after she mastered the skill, she still did not enjoy riding and protested when Julie would suggest family bike rides. Then, one day, out of the blue, she came to me and said, "Daddy, would you like to go bike riding with me?" In that moment my mind was on other things, and I experienced this invitation more as an interruption than as an opportunity. I replied, "No, not now, Kaitlin. I have some things I need to do." She accepted this and went off to ride by herself. Soon afterward, though, I realized just what had happened: our non-bike-riding Kaitlin was actually initiating a father-daughter bike ride, and I had turned her down! I felt terrible and guilty. Fortunately, it didn't discourage her from keeping on with her bicycle riding, but I missed what might have been a priceless adventure.

Of course, there are obviously times when I cannot drop what I am doing unless my child is in real danger or need. But all too often I can get so caught up in my own activities and responsibilities, or just in my own thoughts and feelings, that I can ignore my children when they seek my attention. A thought one of my children may wish to share with me—

"Daddy, did you know that grass is *green?*"——may seem too trivial, too ordinary, too familiar compared to what is going on in my own head at the time. So I respond with disinterest, with brusqueness, even with irritation. At best, I have lost an opportunity to share a moment of wonderment and thereby renew in myself that sense of wonder—something that is very important to one's spiritual life. I have lost an opportunity for connectedness. At worst, I have contributed to the process of shutting down that sense of wonder and sharing in my child.

In that moment, I did not care, and in not caring, the moment fell from the grace it could have had.

Grasping the potential for grace and sacredness in any given moment in the midst of our hectic, overly stimulated, busy days is like catching a soap bubble. It can pop so easily, leaving us feeling damp and disappointed, and with a sense of loss. To keep the bubble whole, we must care and we must take care, but when we succeed, we are rewarded with the pleasure of holding a shimmering iridescence in our hands, a presence of wonder and delight.

In our children are seeds, as shining, beautiful, and graceful as that soap bubble, that, unlike the bubble, can be grasped and strengthened—seeds out of which a spirit of grace and love, beauty and truth, imagination and creativity can develop and grow. When we seek to nourish these seeds, helping our children discover them, claim them, and embody them—in short, when we foster these potentials—then we are parents. When we extend that desire and seek to discover those seeds in the world around us and embrace them with our caring, then we have become mystics.

LAPS

OUR YOUNGEST DAUGHTER MARYN, WHO IS CURRENTLY three years old, is carrying on a fundamental rite performed in their time by each of our children. As soon as either Julie or I sit down, she is in our laps. For that matter, her older sister Kaitlin, who is nine, and her older brother Aidan, who is twelve, also like to climb into our laps on a fairly regular basis. Even John-Michael, who is fifteen and taller than either

Julie or me, will on occasion respond happily to an invitation to sit in our laps, which is a lovely and intimidating experience, as he is all arms and legs and elbows and knees at the moment. Sometimes I even sit on his lap, which is even more intimidating from his point of view!

Not to be left out of the enjoyment, Julie and I sit on each other's laps.

I am convinced that children, especially Maryn's age, see their parents primarily as walking laps. They stalk us, waiting for us to sit down and the lap to appear, and then they pounce. It doesn't matter what I am doing. I can be writing at the computer, reading a book, eating a meal, or just sitting having a rest, and Maryn or Kaitlin—and sometimes Aidan—will be right there, climbing onto me, around me, over me, finally settling down between my belly and my knees. Sometimes I feel like a pillow being fluffed up before being used.

I love it!

Laps are the greatest invention in the world, and I'm forever grateful to the Beloved for making them possible. Horses and elephants, otters and lions have lots of lovely attributes, but they don't have laps. A lap is the warmest, snuggliest, coziest, most loving place in the world; it is a fount of healing, soothing, comfort, reassurance, and wisdom. When they are small, I read to my children on my lap, so it is a portal to worlds of adventure, imagination, learning, and fun as well.

A lap is a parent's best friend, a tool of transformation that would make any magician green with envy. When one or more of the kids is cranky, hurt, crying, angry, or depressed, miracles of healing and upliftment can be initiated with five little words: "Come sit on my lap." Often that's all it takes: a lap, a cuddle, some loving silence together, and presto! Everything is better!

Never mind a course in miracles. What the world needs is a course in laps!

As you may gather, we are a lap-intensive family, hampered only by the fact that there are two parents (with big, multipurpose laps) and four children. But we never let ourselves be limited by scarcity, so when necessary I have been known to have all four kids on my lap at once.

Laps are wellsprings of caring and fostering. A book of instructions for parenting could easily begin, "Step One: Sit down and make a lap." A lap is a symbol and expression of accessibility, of being open and available. Making a lap is like hanging out a shingle saying, "The doctor is in." It's like seeing a welcome sign in the window of your favorite shop.

If I had to sum up my mystical theology in four words, they would be these: God is a lap.

In spiritual circles these days, I often run across the idea that we are each God, creating our own realities. This is not an image I buy into, at least not as it is popularly presented. What I observe is that when people do claim their sacredness in this way, it is usually in terms of power. In our culture we generally equate God with power, so when a person says, "I am god," the implicit subtext is: "Therefore, I am powerful." What he or she is probably not meaning is: "Therefore, I am a lap."

From this mystic's point of view, the essential attribute of the sacred is not power but love. It is perhaps very male and very patriarchal to see God exclusively as the omnipotent creator of universes, the maker and shaker of worlds; I believe it is bad mysticism. A more fundamental understanding to me sees the one presence that is unconditionally, universally, intimately accessible in an inviting and open-hearted way. It is not at the top of a hierarchy, not at the end of years of mystical or spiritual training, but all around us and within us, available to us every moment, no matter who we are or where we are or how well we are doing or how badly we have screwed up. It is accessible precisely because it is there where we are, ready when we are, waiting only for us to slow down, pause, and give our attention to its presence within our lives in whatever way it suits us to do so.

The idea of myself as the creator of my reality is simply not that useful for me—partly because it doesn't take into account the co-creative nature of reality and the fact that other influences and people also shape the world I experience (something any parent can readily attest to!), partly because it encourages a manipulative approach to my life, and partly because it sets up a condition of separation and distance between myself and my reality. I find it more useful to say that I am unconditionally accessible to my reality, that I am the lap of my reality—the seat in which anything in my life can come to be held in my awareness, my love, and my understanding. In my accessibility, my lapness, I become the point of healing, of transformation, and of energy for my reality. Responsibility and fostering spring from the power of my lap.

Being accessible to the world and its challenges—being a spiritual lap that can embrace and hold others in an atmosphere of peace and comfort—is what a person should mean if he or she says, "I am God." Being a lap when that is required is part of the territory of being sacred, just as it is of being a parent. In fact, if I wanted to make a declaration of personal responsibility, power, love, accessibility, and creativity, I would simply say, "I am a Parent!"

Thinking about laps is also useful in suggesting ways to connect with the sacred. Unless you are *very* young, it is hard to be in a lap and be running or jumping at the same time. Laps are places to sit, to be still, to find a moment's respite.

A majority of the training in various spiritual practices is not so much about how to find the sacred as about how to become still enough to recognize the sacred that is already around us and within us. Learning how to sit still, as any parent knows, is a good prerequisite for being in a lap. And becoming still is a choice we can make. There are techniques like counting to ten, watching the breath, and meditating that can help. Ultimately, I choose whether to be in stillness or to be in reaction to the stimulation and dramas around me. That choice, to do what it takes to be still, to enter the lap, is what is most important; without it, the techniques will not work.

With four kids (even with less), there are times when all chaos breaks loose. Everyone wants something at the same time, everyone starts competing with each other for Julie's or my attention, everyone gets snappy and cranky and out of sorts, there is yelling and crying, gnashing of teeth and rending of garments. Often in those moments, Julie and I may not be feeling so centered and together either. Every parent knows some variant of this scenario. It is in these moments that either Julie or I—or preferably both of us—must choose to breathe deeply and project calmness. Metaphorically and often physically we must create lap-space, an energy that is warm and soothing and embracing. We must, in those moments, ignore or set aside our own feelings of chaos. Out of the spirit of our caring, we must choose to concentrate on bringing calm into the situation, becoming the still center—the lap—in which a more harmonious energy can take shape. (We can always go off by ourselves and scream later!)

The spirit of the lap is the spirit of caring and love and fostering within each of us. That spirit is our connection with the sacred. When we invoke that spirit, however simply, we invoke the sacred. We make ourselves accessible to the Beloved.

This principle is expressed in an ancient mystical law that I just made up:

To discover God, make a lap.

LISTENING

ONE EVENING WHILE HOSTING A PARTY OF CLOSE
friends, we had broken up into smaller conversational
groups of two or three people each while our various children played with each other in different rooms of the house.
My oldest daughter, Kaitlin, who was three at the time, had
come into the living room and was sitting watching the
adults. One of our friends saw her, went over and sat next to
her, and asked her how life was going.

Of all my children, Kaitlin is in some ways the most serious and straightforward. Discovering an adult who had sat down to listen to her, she took the invitation seriously and began to answer his question in some detail. As she went on, I could see he hadn't expected to be engaged in such an in-depth conversation. I noticed his eyes glaze over as his thoughts began to wander. After a moment, Kaitlin realized too that he had zoned out and was no longer listening to her. Indignant, she reached over and knocked three times on his forehead, saying, "Hello! Anyone in there?"

Listening is obviously a vital skill in life. It is how we connect with each other, how we learn, how we build communion and community. It is how we express our caring. It is what we do in laps. A great deal of the world's suffering could be alleviated if we listened deeply and compassionately to each other. For listening is the act of entering the skin of the other and wearing it for a time as if it were our own. Listening is the gateway to understanding.

Because I am partly deaf, the legacy of an encounter with particularly aggressive measles when I was six years old, I must pay attention and listen closely when people speak to me. Otherwise, what they say often comes across as a jumble of sounds. So developing listening skills has been important to me.

Few things teach listening as well as being a mystic or being a parent.

The task, and joy, of a mystic is to listen for the stirrings of the sacred in the world and the presence of soul. What the mystic seeks to hear is not a message or even a sound. It is something more subtle and less glamorous. The "hearing" of a mystic is not really auditory at all but more a deeply focused yet widely extended attentiveness. The mystic "hears" in the way a compass "hears" the north or a piece of iron "hears" a magnetic field. The mystic hears the field of life and sacredness within and around herself. He feels the resonance of that field in his being and is drawn into it, becoming a part of it.

A mystic hears through that act of becoming; a mystic hears through a resonance of unity.

What she hears is the flow of life interacting with the forms of life. It is like hearing the explorations of a seed as it seeks the sunlight: hearing the sound of the plant as it moves through the soil to the surface, pushing aside the earth in its way; hearing the thrust of will and life, of desire and direction, of unfoldment and emergence that lie behind that movement.

That is what a mystic hears, finding the correspondence of that thrust, that impulse, that energy, within himself and thus becoming part of it.

For a mystic, the act of hearing is also an act of loving. It is an act of blending and moving with life, discovering where it wants to go and how to bring it forth in a release of desire and creativity.

When I think of the kind of listening that promotes such hearing, I think of a tracker in the wilderness. She allows the boundaries between herself and the forest to become permeable and becomes one with her surroundings, senses fully extended—not in a sharp, focused, laserlike beam, but like a net, spread evenly all around to catch the faintest tremor of presence. Such listening is an embracing, enfolding attentiveness.

At the heart of such listening is silence. Indeed, the cultivation of good listening in any situation is also the cultivation of an inner silence, for I cannot hear what my world is saying if I am chattering unceasingly to myself.

As a parent, I may practice the same kind of listening. Children, especially infants and toddlers, cannot always tell you directly what is on their minds or what they are feeling. Until they develop a command of language, they use a variety of signals, from body language to sounds, to communicate their needs. To understand my children, I had to listen beyond words and verbal communication; I had to pay attention in a way that took me out of myself and into their world.

I discovered, like many other parents I have talked with, that if I listened with my being and not just my ears, I knew within myself what my child was trying to communicate. An image would arise, or an impulse, or a stirring, and some part of me knew. I had listened past my skin and into the life of my child. What mystic could ask for better training than that?

I found that this inner listening worked best when I did not project my own ideas of what a child is or should be upon my child but let his or her own being speak to me. When I was a new father, I unconsciously thought of John-Michael as a blank slate waiting to receive the wisdom and learning I would impart to him. I very quickly learned that each child is a unique soul, a new life with its own priorities, its own capabilities, and its own innate direction and wisdom. My parenting greatly improved when I learned to listen to Johnny as fully and attentively as I expected him to listen to me, and when I was also willing to be changed by what I heard.

Listening changes us. We can hardly enter the skin of another and return unaffected. The change can be very minor, but it can be major as well. If I truly hear what you are saying to me, then it may alter my conception of you and of myself. I may have to let go of some preconceptions.

As I mentioned before, the seduction involved in being a parent is the lure of power and authority, and when one gets caught up in that, one can become hierarchical in one's thinking. The parent is at the top—the source from which wisdom, instruction, commands, and goodies flow downward to the children in a one-way flow. Of course, if I fall into that role, I may stop listening.

It is an axiom of my parenting style that if I want my kids to listen to me, I must listen to them. Just as important, if I want them to change because of what they hear, then I must be willing to change because of what they tell me. That is good parenting, but it is also good mysticism in my book, since in a holistic universe, insight, wisdom, and the spirit of God can come at any time from any direction. Furthermore, listening is by nature a co-creative act from which new possibilities can arise. Why not realize that my children are as much my partners in this process as any adult could be?

If I wish to foster, I must listen. How can I assist that which seeks to emerge if I don't first ascertain accurately what it is? How can I raise my children unless I have a sense of who I am raising, a sense of the spirit that is stirring within their bodies?

In this process, the mystic may have it easier than the parent, for the mystic almost by definition approaches his fostering with humility. How else is one to listen to the presence of the sacred except with humbleness and a willingness to be changed by what one hears? A parent is not always equally humble before the miracle that is the life of her child. We may respect other adults, but children can easily become the Rodney Dangerfields of life. Precisely because they are our children and we have a sense of having created them, and because they are so dependent on us for everything they need (especially in the early years), we can feel proprietary and condescending in a way we might not toward another autonomous adult.

Here lies the parental challenge to listening. For while children are not independent, they are their own beings. As parents, we must walk a line between providing adequate and appropriate authority and guidance for them and recognizing that as fellow members of creation, filled with the same spirit as we, *they* also have wisdom and insight from which *we* can benefit and change. In the midst of showing them what to do to become responsible adults, we must listen as they tell us who they are and who we are as well.

But parents have one big reward. In listening to, raising, loving, and co-creating with our children comes the joy of seeing new realities emerge right before our eyes. What may be abstract for a mystic becomes flesh and blood for the parent as the fruits of listening take shape and form in the bodies of our families and the growth of our children.

ALIENS

GROWING UP ON A UNITED STATES AIR BASE IN
Morocco in the early fifties, my primary source of entertainment was movies. Happily, our house was separated only by
a wide grassy field from a large Quonset hut that served as
the community center, restaurant, and movie theater for the
dependents' side of the base. On a Saturday afternoon, I
could walk across the field and, for ten cents, enter this

building with its dark, cool, cavelike environment and be transported to wonderful worlds of imagination.

My favorite movies were those in which the Earth was invaded by ravening alien hordes in cheesy costumes and the fate of humanity rested on the shoulders of a lone, pipe-smoking, visionary scientist and his girlfriend. (The girlfriend was almost always the screaming target of said aliens' attentions.) The alien invasion genre of movies has seen a comeback recently, but even with millions of dollars in cool special effects, the modern movies don't quite capture the zaniness and tension and sheer, seat-bouncing fun of their matinee predecessors. (Of course, the fact that I am forty-plus years older now could have something to do with that.)

What always puzzled me was why these aliens would travel hundreds of light-years to Earth simply to steal our women. This theme wove through many of the pulp science fiction stories of the forties and fifties. What was it about earthly females that gave them the allure of Swiss chocolate for aliens from galaxies far and near? At the age of ten, it was one of those impenetrable mysteries of the feminine. Fortunately, it took up only enough screen time to create a personal motivation for the hero to do what we all really went to these movies to see: the kicking of alien butt.

But suppose it were not all fiction? Suppose millions of aliens did invade our world? Unable to speak any human language, these beings are nonetheless capable of amazing feats of mental and physical prowess. They behave in ways incomprehensible to ordinary logic. Upon arrival, these beings immediately seize our females, brainwashing them into becoming their slaves, demanding their constant attention, and using them for purposes of pleasure and nourishment. Suppose we males are helpless to stop them, suffering from a similar mind enslavement that forces us to stand idly by, watching and even helping this takeover of our women?

I am here to tell you that this is happening right now, all around us, straight out of the tabloid headlines. The aliens are here.

We call them Children.

Think about it. From birth to age seven or so, children *are* performing amazing feats of physical and mental development. They are learning to correlate their senses with their world and their bodies; they are learning to eat, to crawl, to walk, to talk. In order to do this, they are taking in and processing information about their world at a rate unequaled by almost any adult. Brain cells are growing, synapses are forming, and mental patterns are being laid down with incredible complexity and efficiency. The child is a voracious learning machine, deeply engaged with his world.

As for monopolizing the attention of our women, just ask any new father how much time his wife spends with him.

Of course, our children are not really aliens, but I have used this metaphor over the years to stress a point about communication. It is all too easy to regard our children as incomplete, unfinished adults and therefore treat them with less seriousness and respect than we might another adult . . . or an alien visitor.

Children are not incomplete or unfinished. They are fully functioning organisms just as they are. The fact that they are growing and changing and will gain even greater ability to function in the world is part of the definition of childhood (and of adulthood, but we tend to forget that). Knowing they will be someone more mature tomorrow, with more experience and greater wisdom and judgment, does not detract from their current competency, or the power of who they are today.

For example, children have amazing oral memories, the kind of memory I, for one, have lost because I rely so much on written and visual records. With each of my children, I discovered, like so many parents before me, that all I had to do was read a story once or twice and he or she knew it word for word. This was unfortunate for me when, during bedtime readings, I might want to shorten the story because I was weary or edit and change it for my own amusement. The inevitable result was some form of the following dialogue:

OUTRAGED CHILD: (*voice raised in protest*) "No, no, Daddy. That's *not* how it goes! Read it right!"

WEARY, BEMUSED FATHER: "How do you know? I've only read it to you once before."

CHILD: (*exasperated*) "It goes like this . . ." (Child recites accurately several lines of text from memory. Homer would have been proud.)

This becomes particularly problematic when I make up bedtime stories on the spot, as I sometimes do. The next night, my child will ask me to repeat it, but I may have forgotten just how I told it, leaving out key phrases or character descriptions. But I can always depend on my child to correct me.

As an adult and parent, it is easy for me to fall into the trap of thinking of myself as the expert and teacher, and miss the fact that my children may have abilities that are superior to my own, even at an early age. I remember one day when Aidan, who was about seven, came to ask me to make him a paper hat by folding a single piece of paper. The instructions for doing so were in the Sunday funnies that day. He handed me paper and the directions with every confidence that his wonderful, magnificent, capable dad would have no problem whipping up the paper hat. Little did he know that when it comes to following these kinds of directions and constructing something, I am a total disaster. Finally, after twenty minutes of trying to decipher the devilishly incomprehensible diagrams and having my resulting paper hats fall apart as soon as Aidan put them on, he went and got his older brother. Johnny good-naturedly came over, took the paper away from me, said, "Here, Dad, let me help," and proceeded to transform it into the best paper hat Aidan could want.

In my parenting, I try not to measure my children against adult standards but to appreciate them in the context of their developmental stage. Seen that way, each child, whatever his or her age, is generally engaging his or her world as fully and competently as I do, and often more so, with greater passion, openness, and delight than I can always muster. They do not have the knowledge base that I do, and they may not process information in the same way (though they can be every bit as logical—just try reasoning with a five- or six-year-old about bedtime), but they are thinking, feeling, acting, and interpreting their world just as I do. And if their logic sometimes seems a bit skewed, well, a visitor from Mars might not think the way I do, either.

Besides, from a mystical perspective, *I* am still in *my* childhood; my knowledge base and my way of thinking are limited by my three-dimensional, physical point of view. Adulthood is a very relative term when one takes the spiritual realms into account as well as the physical ones!

Thinking of my children as aliens is not about their strangeness as much as about my own attitudes and attentiveness. It is a parable about communication. Can I listen to and pay attention to my children with the same respect that I would bring to a first contact situation with an extraterrestrial visitor (or another adult, for that matter)? Can I broaden my conception of childhood beyond meaning "incomplete" to meaning "a competent entity at a different stage of development from me"?

Certainly, if I were communicating with an alien, I would make allowances for differences. I would suspend my assumptions and not expect the other to behave as I do. I would be open to the unexpected. While my task might be to instruct it in the ways of the human world, I would not assume that it was a blank slate, ignorant and unformed until I told it what to think and do. I would recognize that it had its own way of thinking, its own intelligence, its own logic, however strange or different from my own. And if this being came up with some erroneous insights about the human condition and life on Earth, I wouldn't assume that it was stupid or incompetent, only that it was struggling to amass and refine its knowledge base as it tried to understand the complexity of an entirely new world.

Especially, I would know that this being embodied mystery and wonder. I would not project my own attitudes, opinions, and ways of thinking onto it. I would come to the encounter prepared to learn as well as to teach, expecting that each of us had something important to contribute to the other.

I bring this attitude—the perspective of a "first contact specialist"—to my interaction with my children. It neither romanticizes nor glamorizes the condition of childhood and its particular perspectives. It does not say my child is a little adult in disguise. It does not say that my child is my equal in knowledge, wisdom, and skill where the world is concerned. But it does acknowledge that my child has knowledge and wisdom and skills different from my own, and that out of them he or she is capable of seeing things and making connections that I may miss. It does allow me to approach my child as an equal in the process of learning about our world.

As a young child, John-Michael struggled with dyslexia, which made it challenging for him to learn to read and write. For someone like myself for whom reading and writing is a major part of life, this was very troubling. But I learned to recognize his other abilities. For example, he has a wonderful capacity to grasp structural relationships and the way things work, far beyond any such capability I have. One evening, John-Michael sat down and put together a rather complex Lego castle. He worked on it right through the evening and had it finished before his bedtime. After we tucked him in, Julie and I examined it and realized that he had constructed it exactly in reverse. Putting this castle together presented no problem for him, but because of his dyslexia he had created a mirror image of the way it was supposed to be without even thinking about it. I saw this not as a problem but as the sign of a wonderful intelligence at work that just happened to see the world a bit differently from the way I did.

From a mystical point of view, we are all first contact specialists all the time. We are each emissaries from our own unique worlds of thought, feeling, and perception, and we are always meeting each other as if for the first time, appearances of familiarity notwithstanding. Yes, my wife and my children look like the same people whom I knew the day before, but are they really? What new thoughts or feelings have arisen since I last saw them? What new ideas? What potentials are bubbling near the surface that weren't there before? How will I know unless I am sensitive to the newness that is always there in each of us?

We are each slices of God, pieces of the infinite, of the primal Mystery. How can we afford not to contact each other, whatever our age, our relationship, or our station in life, with wonderment, respect, and a sense of new possibilities? A mystic strives to meet all of life with this attitude. A parent could do worse than to engage with his or her child from the same perspective.

FIELDS

I ASKED MY NINE-YEAR-OLD, KAITLIN, WHAT SHE thought a family was. She paused for a moment, then said, "A family is a mom and a dad and kids. That's a good family." Then she thought about how her oldest brother John-Michael had been teasing her, and she added, "Another kind of family is a mom, a dad, some kids, and a teenager. That's the kind of family you don't want!"

Unfortunately for Kaitlin, in one more year, Aidan will be thirteen, and then she'll have two older teen brothers. On the bright side, she will become a teenager herself in four years, which will undoubtedly transform her perspective on what makes a good family. Perhaps with that in mind, she said to me later, "Daddy, actually Johnny's a good teenager, really cool!"

Families come in all shapes and sizes and configurations, but there is one thing that is probably common to all of them: they turn out different from what we imagined at the beginning. Like any living being, they grow in all kinds of unpredictable ways, some desirable and, perhaps, some not. They are not like Lego kits that come with instructions for assembly and pieces that fit precisely where we want them to, though sometimes—especially as new parents with lots of ideas and preconceptions but not much experience yet— we can forget that. Certainly, in the first few months of my own parenting, there were times when I tried to fit us all into some predetermined images and roles, only to realize that that led to controlling, not fostering. In the dynamics of human relationships, the best-laid plans, in the immortal words of Robert Burns, can definitely "gang aft aglay." In the military, they have a saying that the finest battle plans in the world last only as long as it takes to make contact with the enemy. This might be paraphrased for parents to say that the best family plan often lasts only as long as it takes for the baby to come home from the hospital and grow a little.

But what do you expect when you let aliens into your house?

In the new sciences, which study the complex relationship between order and chaos, life is described as a quality emerging from the "edge of chaos"—a boundary between chaos and randomness, on the one hand, and order, on the other. Too much chaos, and everything dissipates; life cannot form or hold a structure that would allow it to exist; too much order, and life coagulates into a dense, closed system, a deadening, stultifying structure. Instead, what gives rise to life is a dynamic interplay between chaos and order, a constant falling into and out of equilibrium.

Parents know all about the edge of chaos. It is where our children take us much of the time. Yet it is at this edge that healthy families develop. As our children grow, we quickly learn about the tug-of-war between randomness and freedom on the one side and structure and discipline on the other. A good parent realizes that going too far to the extreme in either direction, either into a rigid order or a diffuse permissiveness, is in no one's best interest. A successful family will have discovered how to creatively balance on that edge.

How does a parent go about that?

A hint. It's not something parents can do all by them-selves.

When I was a child in Morocco, my family became friends with a refugee family who had been high wire acrobats. The circus for which they had worked had broken up during the Second World War; fleeing the Nazis, they had eventually ended up in Casablanca. There they were training their chil-dren and putting together a new act in the hope of traveling to America. One of their stunts was for two people to walk a tightrope with a pole between them, fastened to each of their shoulders, and with a third person walking back and forth along this pole. In such a situation, each acrobat has to both monitor his own center of gravity and be responsive to the center of gravity of the whole trio, which is shifting as everyone changes positions. In effect, what is moving across the wire is a composite entity.

In a family, the situation is similar. When we think of a family, we usually think of its members as Kaitlin did—a dad, a mom, some kids, and even a teenager or two—but, especially from a spiritual point of view, it can be equally helpful and accurate to think of it as a single being, a com-posite or group being or even a field of energy.

Part of the new paradigm that is coming into being in our society is a greater awareness of such things as fields and wholes. For three hundred years, in Western culture at least, it has been increasingly common to understand something by taking it apart; we look at the pieces that result, seeing how they work, and then explain the whole in terms of these pieces. In recent years, a new holistic perspective has been developing that more or less reverses this process. We have been learning to see the wholeness of the whole, as it were, and to understand a thing in terms of what it is and how it expresses itself rather than what it is made of. Now, instead of seeing the universe as made up of little things—atoms or subatomic particles, for example—a physicist may see it composed of energy and relationship.

Of course, this has always been the mystical perspective. Walking a mystical path, I have learned to see the world in terms of interacting wholes or interacting connections of energy and presence. So when I see a family or experience my own family, I see both the individuals who are part of it and the energy of the family as a whole. It is a bit like the acrobat being aware of the center of gravity of all the acrobats; it is an awareness of a field that embodies the organization that links, connects, and coordinates the participating individuals.

The nature of that field for my high wire friends was such that no one acrobat was in a key position to determine the balance for all the rest. Many interacting elements determine that balance.

In a similar way, in a family, it is not always the parents who will have the insight or take the action that will maintain a balance or enable the family to take a creative step forward. If I accept that there is a family energy or soul in which every member participates, then at any given moment, any family member could be the key individual who determines the balance for the rest. A parent or child alike could be the key person who says or does just what is needed in the moment.

When it comes to maintaining the balance of the family at the edge of chaos, paying attention to this field is very important.

To cooperate with this family energy requires listening to each other and listening to the spaces between each other, so to speak—listening to the dynamic that is going on in the larger wholeness that embraces all of us. It means being aware of and understanding a child's needs, which may tell you exactly what needs doing to preserve balance. It means listening to a child's words and observations, which sometimes may have more wisdom and insight than we might credit a child with having. In the context of the family soul, everyone is a valuable participant, if not always an equal one.

As a new parent, I used to feel that I had to be a fount of ever-ready wisdom—that I needed to be on top of my parenting, always knowledgeable about what needed to happen for my kids' sakes. In fact, I wasn't always filled with wisdom;

I didn't always know what to do. Lots of times I didn't have a clue, and this would make me feel as if I were failing as a father.

What helped me move beyond this was to realize that I was violating one of my own basic points of view as a mystic. I am both an individual and a participant in a larger wholeness—like light, both wave and particle—and in the context of that wholeness, all the good stuff didn't have to come from just me. It could come from Julie, which I had already acknowledged, but it could also come from my children themselves. And sometimes insight would come just by listening to the sense of the family collective, or considering how it related to the wider world around us.

In this sense, translating a mystical perspective of wholenesses into a perspective of family wholeness proved very helpful. It did not diffuse my responsibility, but I now felt that I had allies in the process of maintaining the balance of the family. I began to pay more attention to the subtleties of mood and atmosphere and to feel the energy of our family in those inner places from which intuition arises.

I realized that if I didn't insist that only Julie or I could have parenting wisdom, I could recognize the times when an important voice of family wholeness and balance could be heard in things my kids would say, questions they would ask, and ideas they would offer. Family meetings are important to us as opportunities when everyone can make contributions, but the "voice of the family" can speak through anyone anytime, so I always try to be open so as to hear it and recognize it when it does.

Even Maryn, at the age of two, responding to some inner prompting, would sometimes seek me out when I was off by myself in another part of the house. I would be feeling depressed, perhaps, or out of sorts for one reason or another, and she would put her arms around me, and say, "It's OK, Daddy, it's OK." Of course, children are sensitive to moods and can be very intuitive about what their parents are feeling or what is going on in the family at large. There is nothing surprising about that. I have experienced such moments with all of my children, as have other parents whom I know.

The point is that at that moment, Maryn was fostering me. The energy of parenting, of nurturing and support, was coming from her to me, and the relative difference in our ages and experiences made no difference. I have seen Maryn do this for her siblings also, and they do it for her and for each other.

In short, while there is an aspect of parenting that is very focused through Julie and me as the responsible adults in the household, there is another aspect that is diffused throughout our whole family, and anyone can manifest it at anytime toward anyone else. To call it "parenting" may be stretching the normal way we use that word; but it definitely inspires us to foster and care for each other, to listen deeply, and to be laps for each other. In my book that is what real parenting is all about.

There is another point to be made about fields. It's important to recognize that they are not like boxes that contain but like configurations that interact, merging and blending with other fields they may encounter. You cannot see, for example, where a magnetic field begins and ends, though you can test it by seeing how far its influence extends. And everything within its influence, everything that can be affected by a magnet, is affected.

In an analogous way, the energy of the family whole is not restricted only to its home, for example, or even to its biological members. Given the right affinity and resonance, others may be part of this field, even at a distance. Their influence within or on the family (or the family on them) may be minor, but it can still be present.

Thus, when I tell someone that he or she is "part of our family," this can literally be true on an inner level. Not that I am then responsible for them or must parent them, but their energy and spirit can be woven into our family in interesting and hopefully helpful ways.

Which raises the question that I asked Kaitlin: What is a family? Who constitutes the family? On a physical level, the answer may be obvious, and, for most practical purposes, that answer is sufficient. But on an inner, spiritual level—the level of the mystic—a family may be larger than we suppose. It may include the land on which our house is built, and the creatures who share that land with us, all embraced in the field of our family's energy. And that field may expand to embrace others, both near and far, with whom we share a bond of love and mutual interest.

In time, we may even learn how to see the world and all humanity as our family, expanding the field of our compassion, our fostering, and our love until no one is excluded.

That would be a very mystical thing to do, indeed!

FAITH

I AM SEATED AT MY DESK WRITING ON A LEGAL PAD. THE room is filled with twilight; the brightest point is a single lamp shining down on the paper in front of me. Behind me, I hear the door open, and I swing around to see who has entered. It is a boy looking to be about eleven or twelve, and he is enveloped in an aura of rich, golden light that glows like a candle flame more brightly as it nears his body. The whole room lights up as if the sun has entered, which is surely a visual pun, for as I stare in surprise at this figure, he says, "I am your son. I want you to know I have no intention of doing the kind of work you do. I am going to be a doctor!" At which point, I wake up.

I had this dream toward the end of our first pregnancy, and I took it as fair warning not to lay any expectations on the new person who was coming into our family. Whoever this person would be, he had his own plans for his own life. The dream was far from prophetic, though. Of all our children, John-Michael so far is the one who shares my intuitive sensitivities, and while he has shown no desire to be a teacher, he does not want to be a doctor, either! His life plan at the moment is to be a commercial pilot. Still, the essence of the dream was to remind me that my children are not clay to be molded or puppets to be dangled but, like all children, come into life filled with their own souls' intents.

Interestingly, this dream also had historical resonances with my relationship with my father, and his relationship with his. When my father was growing up on a farm in Ohio, he wanted to be a medical missionary. His hero was Dr. Albert Schweitzer, whose credo was reverence for all life. In fact, my father has always followed this credo, and it has formed a core element of our family spirituality.

My paternal grandfather, on the other hand, was a successful engineer and inventor; he held several important patents. He had his own laboratory right next to the farmhouse. He was determined that Dad would be an engineer like him. Eventually he won out, and Dad did become an engineer. All the years I have known him, though, my dad has still cherished the dream of serving people and has wondered what his life would have been like if he had followed his original calling.

Reflecting on this struggle in his own life, my father once told me that, unlike his father before him, he would not interfere in my choice of what I would do in my life. He would be there to support me in whatever career I decided to follow.

The opportunity to put his declaration to the test came when I was in college. I had been studying toward a bachelor of science degree with the intention of becoming a molecular biologist. During this period, though, the mystical side of my nature came more and more to the fore, and I realized with some surprise that my own inner calling was not to the laboratory but to pursuing a spiritual work.

The decision to follow this inner calling was far from easy. At least, it meant giving up my scholarships and my life at the university during my junior year, where I was very successful academically. At most, it meant abandoning my goal of becoming a molecular biologist in favor of a very unknown future. How much faith did I have in spirit, anyway?

If it was hard for me, I knew it would be doubly so for my father, who was very proud and supportive of my intention to become a scientist. I talked it over with my mother first, who let me know she was behind me a hundred percent. But I put off telling Dad until I was very sure in myself about the step I was going to take. Finally, one evening I drove home from the dormitory and sat down with him in the living room. I told him that I was planning to drop out of school to go off and be a freelance mystic instead of a research scientist.

To say that he was dismayed would be like saying that it rains in Seattle. I'm sure he thought his only son had gone mad. It would be unfair to say we had a fight, since Dad was too loving for that. But all through that evening, he definitely communicated his bewilderment and concern over my decision, and I communicated the extent of my commitment in return. I'm sure the historical irony of the situation struck us both, for we were replaying the argument he had had with his own father years before—the argument between a spiritual calling and a scientific one.

Finally, he left me alone and disappeared into his bedroom. I sat in the living room for about an hour, wondering what would happen next. Then the bedroom door opened, and Dad came back out. He sat down on the couch in front of me, took my hands in his, and said, "David, I am not happy about this choice you're making, and I don't pretend to understand it, but if you want to be a mystic, then I want you to go out there and be the best damned mystic you can be!" With that he hugged me and went back to bed. Two days later I had packed my car and was on the road to find my new life.

Vice President Hubert H. Humphrey once said that each child is an adventure into a better life, an opportunity to change old patterns and make them new. For me, each parent can be the same thing. My dad was determined to change an old parental pattern of control passed down to him from his father, and he did. He gave me his blessing to follow my own inner calling, and gave himself the ability to move on in new ways. These actions, though, required faith and listening on both our parts.

In the metaphysical and esoteric traditions, it is common to talk about "the soul's intent," the impulse of will and vision that brings a person into life and around which his or her destiny will form. This image can be misleading, for in my experience the soul's intent is not quite the same thing as a goal I might hold in my everyday life. It's generally not like saying, "I am going to buy a new van" or "I intend to be a doctor." The soul's intent in most cases is much less bound to a specific vocation or mission and is much more about the patterns and qualities that a person is called to express. It's as if the soul has a bundle of apples to distribute but doesn't care whether this distribution takes place in a grocery store, through mail order, or by giving them away on the street—as long as the apples get out into the world and are as ripe and nutritious as possible.

So, even though my father did not become a medical missionary, he did become a biological engineer who worked in the medical area. In his relationships with people, he has always been a loving, generous presence to whom people in all walks of life have turned for help, advice, and encouragement. He and my mother have both been emissaries of spirit. My father's life did not take a particular form as he originally envisaged it, but he has distributed the same gifts of spirit—the same apples—as if he had become a missionary.

This inner current of destiny and spirit can take different forms of expression, but its essential character remains inviolate. Trying to force that essence to be something else is violating the core of one's being, like forcing Johnny Appleseed to grow oranges instead.

A friend of mine, Andy Smallman, is the founder of the Puget Sound Community School (PSCS), an alternative school John-Michael attends. This school encourages students to design their own individualized learning programs and involves them in apprenticeships, community service projects, and the Internet in addition to classroom time.

Andy and I occasionally get together for lunch to talk about the school, educational philosophy, how the Mariners are doing, and life in general. During one of these discussions, I asked Andy what was at the heart of his educational vision. He thought for a moment and then said, "Harmlessness. I want a school that does no harm to the students."

He was talking not about physical harm but the kind of harm that comes when children are not allowed to grow in their imaginations and to discover freely who they are. He was talking about the kind of harm that a cookie-cutter approach to education—stamping out each student in an identical mold—can do to the growth of a child's individuality. He was talking about the harm that results when we don't have faith in a child's sense of who he or she is and what he or she wants out of life. Or the kind of harm that results when we diminish a child's sense of faith in himself by telling him what he wants and what he should do rather than listening to what *he* has to say.

Obviously, such an approach must take into account a child's relative immaturity and smaller knowledge base; a child is not left wholly unguided, for that can be another kind of harm. But in Andy's vision as a teacher—and in my vision as a parent—the skill lies in knowing when to advise and when to back off and let the child learn for herself, when to instruct and when to listen. It is an application of respect for your child, and a demonstration of your faith that within him or her is a deeper intelligence that intuits what he or she has to offer the world. Because while that intelligence will need help in achieving its goals, it doesn't need to have its intent circumvented or denied by a parent's own ideas of what a child should be.

Having faith in the currents of destiny and spirit unfolding within one's child is a scary yet essential part of how Julie and I practice parenting. It is scary because we must relinquish control at appropriate moments along the child's path of development. But it is essential because if my child is to grow fully into the promise of her (or his) life, she must engage with her own inner visions and intuitions about who she is and what she wishes to become. It involves listening and cooperation of the most intimate kind.

It involves the kind of listening that is essential to the mystical path. One of the tasks of a mystic is to listen to the energy and essence, the direction and intent, of these inner currents of incarnation within the world and to foster them appropriately. A mystic must discern the core of what seeks to emerge and help it take shape, without imposing on it his own opinion of what it should be. This is not unlike the work of a gardener; she can shape a garden in a variety of ways, but she does not attempt to grow a rose from a tulip bulb or make a cherry tree give forth olives.

One day Kaitlin, who loves horses, came to Julie and told her that she wanted to be a jockey when she grew up. Julie's first thoughts were that it would be difficult being a female jockey in a predominantly male sport, and that she would probably not be the right size as an adult anyway. So she began to discourage Kaitlin from having that vision. But partway through telling Kaitlin why planning to be a jockey was not a good idea, Julie realized with shock that she was arbitrarily putting limits on her that didn't need to be there. So what if it might be a difficult path? Women had followed difficult paths before in pursuing their dreams. Julie felt she was telling Kaitlin to circumscribe her dreams, telling her that she didn't have the power to have a vision and go for it. So Julie immediately stopped and admitted her mistake to Kaitlin. Then, instead, she expressed support for the fact that Kaitlin could be very strong, and that would allow her to do anything she set her mind to.

After that Julie did some research and discovered that there are many female racing jockeys. In fact, two of the most successful raced at Emerald Downs, our local track. She also discovered that Andy Smallman's father had been a sportswriter who specialized in horse racing and knew these women jockeys personally. Through him, Julie arranged for Kaitlin and herself to meet with one of the female jockeys and talk about what would be involved in Kaitlin's pursuing that sport.

In this way, Julie turned an unthinking response of "Oh, no, you shouldn't do that," into a supportive, empowering engagement with Kaitlin's vision. She showed that she was willing to truly listen as Kaitlin explored what her inner voice might be telling her, and gave Kaitlin tools and experiences to evaluate that voice for herself. She had faith that, given the right knowledge, Kaitlin had the power to choose well for herself. Just as important, Julie knew that the very act of holding a vision and working to achieve it was important to any child's growth and self-esteem, even if the details of the vision changed as the child matured.

This is the same challenge that any parent faces: to listen deeply to discern the soul's intent of her child, to listen to its voice as the child grows, and even to stand aside if it seems to take the child in a direction different from her own. Not that a parent should be passive and never provide guidance— not every voice a child hears comes from its deepest purposes—but rather that the parent should become a partner in the child's development, not its sole arbiter. This is to avoid trying to make the cherry tree of the child's soul produce the olives that the parent's heart conceives.

This act of listening requires faith. Even though he disagreed with my choice and could not see the wisdom in it, my father had faith in me and in my judgment. Both he and

Mom had faith in my inner spirit—in its ability to guide me in my life and in my ability to listen to it appropriately.

Faith is a major tool for a mystic. Not blind, unreasoning faith. To surrender one's intellect is like cutting off one leg. Hopping precariously along an inner path on the single leg of emotion is nowhere near as balanced, comfortable, and effective as combining it with the other leg of reasoned thinking and critical discernment.

Faith, to me, is the capacity to be open to the intangible, invisible domains of life. It is the ability to be comfortable in the presence of Mystery. It is the willingness to go where the senses cannot always take us, to appreciate and be open to the realm of energy, and spirit. Since this is the realm in which a mystic does most of her work, to have no faith is to be severely restricted.

Faith is also a domain in which parents work. When I held each of my children as babies, I could feel the spirit within them. But I had no way of knowing whether that spirit would choose to be a doctor or a priest, a writer or a pilot, an actor or a president of the United States. The depths of my children are a mystery waiting to unfold, and, frankly, I like it that way. I don't want to have a particular role in mind that I think they should fulfill, because that gets in the way of listening to what is actually unfolding.

This kind of listening comes very much into play for me

in dealing with John-Michael's education at the PSCS. At the beginning of each quarter, every student plans out his or her individualized curriculum for the next three months or so. Andy believes that children learn best when they are involved in their own educational process and are engaged with what interests them.

This has created heart-stopping moments for me when Johnny has decided that what interests and engages him for a particular quarter has nothing to do with traditional topics like math, history, or English. I come from a strong academic background, as I have mentioned, in molecular biology and had a very structured curriculum. So I hover over my son every quarter, wondering about his freedom to choose and wanting him to take subjects that I think he should take for the sake of his future—or at least those that I would be interested in. And when he doesn't, the need for faith comes in in spades!

But then I reflect on my own path and realize that I am hardly a model of conventionality. I cannot tell John-Michael to be what I wouldn't be. I can just hear the conversation. "Well, son, the fact that I dropped out of college to become a freelance mystic and have been self-employed all these years, even ending up teaching in colleges, is no reason for you not to study math, science, and history and maybe become the scientist I had intended to be!" I could never do it, nor would I want to. Neither the path I chose nor the one I didn't seem to be John-Michael's path.

I also recognize that in the three years that John-Michael has been part of PSCS, he has grown and matured in remarkable ways. He *has* learned his math and his English, but he has also learned how to be his own person, how to know and speak with his own voice. He is far more assured and comfortable with himself and with his differences from others, as well as with his creative power to make choices and shape his future, than I was at his age. At a critical time in his life, the school has been very good for him. It has honored his otherness, and he has learned how to reach within himself and find the resources to shape his life. He is finding his voice.

If I need to have faith in my children, I also need to have faith in myself and in Julie as parents. If I waited to parent until I had all the wisdom and knowledge I felt I needed, I would still be standing by the crib. But babies have a way of growing and cribs of emptying, whether we feel ready or not. So we learn by doing, as well as by studying, sharing, listening, and intuiting.

Parents work with very tangible things: their children's bodies, food, clothes, medicines, and the like. But the most important work that a parent does takes place in intangible realms—realms of love, of forgiveness and faith, of caring and listening. My children are more than their bodies, and if all I do is feed them, clothe them, and keep them physically well, I am only partly fostering. It is in the invisible realm of spirit, mind, and emotion that much of my parenting takes place, and it is in that realm that the soul's intent within each child takes form and is nourished. It is in that realm that I must listen and observe and feel, with faith opening my inner ears, my inner sight, and my inner touch.

Faith creates an open space in which the unexpected, the unpredicted, and, often, the most essential can appear and become known. Faith is the open space in which miracles may occur, the emptied stage that allows new stories to be told, new meanings to unfold, and new futures to be born.

To serve the future and the emergence of new potentials, to "adventure into a better life," to change old patterns and make them new—these are the acts of faith. And it is these acts that shape so much of the work of both parents and mystics.

SELFING

SOMETIMES I SIT AND WATCH MY FOUR KIDS AT PLAY AND am amazed at the rich complexities of personality and behavior that have emerged from Julie and me. In them I can see fragments of ourselves, of our parents, of the kids' uncles and aunts and cousins, even of their grandparents: a blend of familiar features and habits of expression. I can see my dad's smile or Grandpa Roger's chin; there's a gesture like the one Scotty makes, and there's Jamie's thoughtfulness. There are my eyes. There's Julie's nose. But where did Maryn's dimples come from?

These familiar elements can be misleading, for they can obscure the otherness that is also there. The children are so alike, yet so different from each other and from Julie and me. Each of them is unique and irreplaceable, the facets of their personalities creating a particular geometry of being.

Honoring the otherness of one's child is not always easy. Like Professor Henry Higgins in *My Fair Lady,* a parent can easily find himself wondering, "Why can't my children be more like me?" We know ourselves (more or less), but a child is a mystery, a wholly new person who has a combination of characteristics that has never existed before. There may be many similarities and patterns in common with their ancestors, but the child is still unique. So as a parent, I must observe, listen, and explore to see how I am to raise this person. I must be prepared to go beyond my own preferences and habits.

This takes faith, as I mentioned in the last chapter. It is easy for me to have faith in someone who is my clone. Where faith really counts is where it allows me to trust what is different from me.

When my father supported my leaving school, he was expressing his faith in how my self was different from his. He was not saying, "David, you must be like me, or I will not have faith in you." He had faith that my life could unfold successfully in a way different from his. He was honoring my unique self and the life choices that would flow from it. He had faith in my otherness.

This honoring of otherness and selfhood is very much part of the mystical journey. It might not seem so at first glance, since so much is said about "oneness" as the objective of that journey. It might seem that mystics and parents are at two opposite ends of the stick—the ultimate wholeness that underlies all creation on one end and the abundant and delightfully rich diversity that characterizes the physical universe on the other. Traditionally, a mystic seeks to transcend the self, while a parent seeks to enhance the self-development of her children. A mystic seeks to dissolve otherness, while a parent seeks to attune to qualities and particularities that make each child different.

In fact, one might say that a parent is a mystic of the self.

Not that parents wouldn't appreciate a little oneness now and again. Trying, for instance, to cook a meal that will please four children who all have their own preferences and tastes—not to mention what Dad and Mom may like—is a daily exercise in exploring elusive pathways to unity that would challenge any mystic.

The realm in which parents work is not one in which differences dissolve into unity and the self becomes absorbed into a primal oneness. Parents serve in the trenches of differentiation; they labor amid a friction of selves and a pride of egos, all rubbing against each other, conflicting with and learning from the differences that make us each unique. A mystic may deal with universalities, but a parent must deal with particularities.

It is true that one of the hallmarks of mystical experience is a sense of unity, of entering an infinitely inclusive oneness. It is also true that to come to that point, one may first need to surrender attachment to the sense of separateness and even specialness that an individual may feel. But part of the mystical experience for me has also been to see the value of the individual self as a vessel through which that oneness may act in a unique and differentiated way. For the universe is not only a wave of wholeness and spirit, it is also a complex and co-creative interrelationship of particles, individualized bits of sacredness. God is in the details.

As I said earlier, the objective of a mystic, in my experience, is to embody the oneness in the world in a way that serves the incarnational process and emergence of the sacred. This means honoring the differences and uniqueness that create individuality and the specific relationships that individuals form that can foster emergence.

In honoring the otherness of our children, Julie and I see

ourselves as co-creating their personhood with them. A child is not a Galatea to be shaped and brought into being by a Pygmalion; the shaping force is within the child. The self knows, the soul knows, what it wants to become. And the parent is part of that becoming. We provide the genetic framework and the body to begin with, and we provide a physical, mental, emotional, and spiritual environment from which the child will take what she needs. Through the way we lead our own lives, we model the values and traits of character that we feel are important. As parents we are our children's mentors in the craft of "selfing," the art of creating one's own personhood.

As such, one of the most important lessons we offer is in understanding the power and responsibility of choice in the shaping of one's unique self. As much as is possible and in age-appropriate ways, we give our children choices. They are creative parts of the family, after all. We want them to know that, and to learn just what it means to make choices that affect themselves and others, and to understand the consequences. We run the family as a kind of theocratic democracy: everyone gets a say in making family decisions, particularly those that affect all of us, but Julie and I are the goddess and god of the household who have the right to exercise divine intervention and veto power!

We set family rules and limits, and there are consequences that go with breaking them. Julie taught me the power of using logical and natural consequences early in our career as parents, a system she learned from the STEP program (which stands for Systematic Training for Effective Parenting, a program which she uses as the basis for her parent education classes; for further information, see the suggested reading list). In this system, you distinguish between natural, logical, and punitive consequences. The natural consequence of hitting a lamp with a ball, for example, is that it falls over and breaks. The logical consequence for a child is that he might pay to replace the lamp, as opposed to a punitive consequence, which might be that he is spanked or deprived of some privilege.

The system encourages an emphasis on logical rather than punitive consequences in dealing with children, the main difference being that in the former there is a direct connection between the act and the result, while that is not always true for the latter. The punishment a parent inflicts might have no bearing on the nature and severity of the child's infraction, and may be determined solely by the parent's anger. I know. I've been there. (JULIE: "David, why are you throwing out all of Aidan's toys?" ME [*steaming*]: "Because he refused to clean up his room when I asked him!")

A good example of this system at work came one morning when John-Michael decided he would balance a plastic bucket of water on the door into our downstairs hall to see what would happen when someone (me) unsuspectingly opened that door. He was going through a phase of devising and setting such clever traps around the house. It gave us all a crash course in being alert to the dangers in one's environment that would have made a Navy SEAL proud. Julie had already told Johnny not to do the bucket of water experiment, but the urge for scientific exploration and mayhem won out, so he went ahead anyway. As it happened, I did come along and open the door, and the bucket did fall down, but it and the water missed me. Obviously, mystics have divine protection.

As you might expect, I found this near encounter with a concussion and drowning a source of profound amusement and delight and hauled Johnny upstairs to find some way of suitably expressing my sentiments. (Wistful visions did pass through my mind of my grandfather making my dad go and cut a hickory switch that would be the instrument of his punishment, but I didn't think one of our pine branches would be quite the same. Besides, I don't believe in corporal punishment, though there have been moments . . .)

At this point Julie intervened, considering herself the wronged one since it was she Johnny had disobeyed (though, I argued reasonably, it hadn't been her head on the block, as it were). She assigned the logical consequence, which was that Johnny had to take towels and clean up all the water that had soaked into the hallway carpet and then wash the towels. Score one for logical consequences. It took Johnny the better part of the morning to do this (there had been a *lot* of water in that bucket), and when he was done, he was so tired, he swore he would never do something like that again. In fact, after that, all the traps disappeared (I think).

Making choices and taking responsibility for their consequences are powerful tools for teaching children about the craft of selfing. After all, we shape ourselves and our world by our choices. They are the way we become co-creators.

IMAGES

I NO LONGER REMEMBER JUST WHAT JOHN-MICHAEL did that prompted my anger. I do remember standing in the kitchen, morphing into Zeus mode, and preparing my thunderbolts and lightning. But before the wrath of Olympus descended, a little voice in my head said, "Who is really angry here?" The question so intrigued me that whatever I had been going to say never got out of my mouth. Instead, much to

Johnny's puzzlement, I just stood there, examining what I was feeling. As I did so, I realized that the anger was coming from an image that said, "This is a time when a father is supposed to get angry," but what I really felt wasn't anger at all, it was humor.

This incident made me pay more attention to what was going on in my parenting. I started to realize just how much of my fathering was influenced by my images of what a father did and how a father should be. It didn't matter where these images had come from. Some obviously came from my experiences with my own father, some came from observing friends who were parents, and some came from books or television shows (I was always a fan of *Father Knows Best*).

There is nothing original or surprising about this. We all model ourselves on others to some degree, and we all draw on a repertoire of images and subpersonalities that we can don, masklike, at appropriate moments. Images can be useful, not unlike a "macro" on my computer: a pre-programmed command that I can initiate simply by hitting a particular key. Such images provide a simplistic logic that automatically links perception and response, eliminating the need to really see or think about what is going on. One of my children is acting up at the dinner table, and my Ideal Dad Image says fathers should reprimand children who act up at the dinner table. So, without having to think about it, I get angry and tell my child to stop misbehaving. But the intervention of the image of what a father should do in such an instance denies me the opportunity both to investigate more deeply why the child is acting up and to choose from a variety of responses.

For example, one evening Aidan began hooting at the dinner table, mimicking the cry of whatever creature might result from the mating of a screech owl with a steam locomotive. I have no idea why he started doing this, except that it must have seemed fun at the time (and there have been times when I've felt an impulse to hoot as well, which undoubtedly tells you more about the Spanglers than you wanted to know). His three siblings did not hesitate to follow his example. At this moment, Ideal Dad would say, "Hey, we do not hoot over our food. Please be quiet!" I certainly felt the impulse to say just that. But, as far as I could see, no harm was being done. We weren't dining out at the Four Seasons (but then, we never dine out at the Four Seasons) or at McDonald's or anywhere else public, and dinner conversation had been rather sparse that night anyway. So I started to hoot with them, and Julie quickly followed suit. Soon we were all branching off into our own individual squeals, brays, whistles, howls, shouts, and yodels that would have done the musicians of Bremen proud. It definitely turned a flat evening into a raucous, energetic, delightful one. But it's not the path Ideal Dad would have chosen.

We all have our images, little inner movies of who we should be, how we should act, what we should say. To say that they can control us is giving them more power than they deserve. They seem strong and compelling, but they are no more than wisps of imagination. We believe them to be more substantial, more necessary than they are. Once I see them as tools and not as facets of identity, then I can use them or not as I decide.

It's coming to that place of recognition that is challenging. There is an alluring convenience to putting our lives on autopilot and letting our internal images tell us what to do. They are the labor-saving devices of the psyche. Particularly as parents, there are so many demands on our lives beyond just our children, and time always seems at a premium. Plugging into the Ideal Mom or Ideal Dad Image and letting it run the show is much easier than having to be clearly attentive to each moment; easier than having to put out that extra energy to truly *see* just what is the appropriate response for this child at this moment, whether it is anger, humor, comforting, discipline, or just silence.

I don't know how it is for others, but I know when I am surrendering my authority to an image. I can feel its persona, its mask and energy, settling about me; I feel subtle changes in my facial muscles, and my body alters its stance. Of course, this happens very quickly. But the mystical path is nothing if not one in which you choose to observe what is going on within yourself in order to arrive at deeper self-knowing. So I have come to recognize the symptoms.

I have learned to step back when I feel habit taking over. I relax my face and move my body into a different, more neutral posture. I empty my mind (as in counting to ten, a wonderfully useful, ancient mystical exercise for achieving calm and presence in the moment!) and then refocus my attention outward onto the situation. The challenge is not really that I am taking on the image. The challenge is finding the energy to resist the easy, automatic path the image offers. The challenge is to be very present and attentive and give myself an opening to find a different response if necessary.

For the first few years that I was a parent, I struggled with the images I carried of what a father should be like. Some of these images were good and helpful. Since I was raised by very loving and involved parents, my parenting images tend to be open, supportive, and quite positive. But for all the guidance they can offer, they still are only images—memories, and interpretations of past events. They are no substitute for real-time appreciation of and insight into the moment that is unfolding right now. They are best used as advisors, not decision-makers.

Because I am an only child, I felt familiar and confident

while I was the parent of an only child. This was a situation I was used to, and, if needed, I could call on memories of how my own dad handled me to help me with John-Michael. I was comfortable with the images I had inherited. But even then, I overstated to myself the extent of their usefulness, for John-Michael is not me. We are different selves. Our personalities, the circumstances of our births, and the environment of our early childhoods are not the same. Some of the ways Dad adapted to me and my needs would be inappropriate for Johnny, and my son has had needs I didn't have. But even with these important differences, I still felt I was in familiar territory as a father.

When Aidan came along I began to panic, for I had no images at all for fathering brothers. This feeling only worsened when Kaitlin was born three years later, and I was faced with fathering a daughter. What was I going to do? What did I need to do? Fortunately, Julie comes from a family of four children that is almost a mirror of our own, so I had her experience to draw on.

Then one day it dawned on me that I was coping with the situation. I was relaxed and at ease with parenting more than one child at once, and I had developed skills that my own father had never needed. I suddenly felt very free from the images of my past when I realized that they didn't correspond to my own situation. I didn't have to measure up to my dad's legacy. It had not been diminished in any way; it was simply different.

But that is true for every parent. Each child, each family, is different from what has gone before. No image based on any one parent's experience is going to match up one hundred percent with the needs and characteristics of any other parent's situation. These images of how to parent, of what it means to be a father or mother, can be extremely useful (or very toxic, in circumstances where a person suffered from parental abuse and neglect), but they will never fit exactly. They cannot take the place of one's awareness and sensitivity, one's energy in the moment. It may well be that the response to a child that is needed is something no one has thought of before, or at least something different from what one's own parents might have done.

This need to detach from the images within us is also very much part of the mystical path. In the case of a mystic, the images are those of the sacred: images of what and who God is, what spirit is, what life is all about. But those images can stand in the way of an authentic experience of the sacred in the same way that my Ideal Dad Image can prevent my being an authentic parent. Having an image of God and experiencing the sacred are two different things—just as an image of my wife or my children is not the same as the actuality of my wife or my children. The map is not the same as the territory. However helpful a map may be, we will not understand or know the territory unless we put away the map and actually explore it for ourselves.

So much of the work in a mystical discipline involves stripping away images in order to see and blend with the deeper reality. It is a task of discarding masks. But this emphasis can be misleading, for in fact, the masks themselves are not the problem. The real lesson to be learned, if the mystic goes deeply enough, is how and why we make these masks, when they are appropriate to wear and when they are not. What a mystic learns is that the compelling, illusory, and obstructive power lies not in our images themselves but in our desire for an easy way out—for a way of relating to life that doesn't require so much energy, so much attentiveness, so much engagement, and so much love. What the mystic struggles with is the tendency to live on automatic pilot— the lazy attraction of sleepwalking and the seeming safety of habit.

Every good parent knows that his or her child is a unique individual who requires more than a by-the-book approach. You don't have to be a mystic to understand this. But the essence of this understanding is the attitude with which a mystic approaches the world in striving to discover the essence within things—to go beyond the surface, beyond the apparent, beyond the automatic. Both our selfhood and our communion as parents and children require a commitment of awareness that is insufficiently present when we act from image and not from self. There certainly may be tasks one can do in a repetitive and habitual way, but neither parenting nor mysticism is among them.

EMERGENCE

As a child, I used to like watching my dad work in the kitchen. While my mother was a wonderful cook, my father viewed cooking as his art form, and he had a gourmet's gift for it. A friend of ours who was psychic once told him that in a previous life he had been a taster in the court of an ancient king, responsible for detecting the slightest traces of poison in the royal meals. Whether she was kidding or not I never knew, but there is no doubt that my dad could have ably filled such a job in this life. Give him a taste of something, and he can rattle off its ingredients as if reading a report from a chemical analysis lab.

When I was a youngster, Dad particularly liked to prepare large meals for our friends. These feasts were all-day affairs. My dad would begin cooking early in the morning and carry on throughout the day. He particularly loved preparing Greek and Arabic dishes, a legacy of the six years we lived in Morocco. He rarely depended on a recipe, preferring to rely on his own creativity. Like a medieval alchemist, he would reach into his extensive collection of spices and herbs, drawing out a pinch of this and a sprinkle of that for the various pots and pans he had going on the stove. All day long he would dice, slice, simmer, stir, and taste. No king was ever happier in his castle than my father was in his kitchen.

Around midafternoon, friends would begin arriving, and we would set up a long table in the living room. There would be conversation and music, usually Greek or Arabic to go along with whatever meal Dad was cooking, and we would mingle until word came down that dinner was ready. Then we would gather at the table like acolytes before an altar, reverent and expectant. Wearing his chef's hat like a cardinal's miter, Dad would appear bearing each entrée as if it were the Host itself. Every morsel would be arranged colorfully and artistically on each plate, for presentation was important to my father. Then, when all were served, Dad would sit, and we would feast.

My dad tried several times to teach me to cook, but always unsuccessfully. It wasn't lack of interest on my part; the fact is that I rank among the culinarily challenged. I have hardly any sense of smell and consequently not much sense of taste. While I have always appreciated the artistry of my dad's cooking, I'm sure I have never experienced all its subtlety the way others have. I'm equally sure his gourmet soul must have cringed many times when he saw me putting liberal globs of ketchup (one of the things I *can* taste) on his creations, though he graciously never said a word.

Still, I was fascinated by my father's herbs and spices, by the intuitive way he always seemed to know which one to add, and when, and how much. And I very much wanted to cook like Dad did. One day when I was about fourteen, while home alone (a phrase guaranteed to send shivers up any parent's spine), I decided that I would try to prepare my own feast for the family. I no longer remember anything about that meal, except that it was astonishingly inedible and had to be thrown away quickly before the plates dissolved. But I think I used a bit of every spice Dad had in the kitchen on the theory that if one was good, many would be better. After that my cooking lessons ground to a halt.

Even if I didn't learn cooking at my father's elbow, I learned something else (besides dishwashing prowess—Dad's philosophy seemed to be "Let no pan go unused!"). I observed that when Dad cooked, he did not simply add things together to make a meal, no matter how artfully. He allowed the meal to emerge. Not that he didn't have a sense of what he wanted to make (though sometimes he would just start combining things to see what would happen). It was more that in order to arrive at the result he wanted, he had to surrender some measure of his control and dominance as the chef.

I remember talking with a woodcarver once at a craft fair. His work was excellent, and I asked him how he went about achieving his effects. He said simply, "I let the wood tell me what it wants to become. The carving is already there. I just let its soul emerge through my fingers."

This is what Dad would do with his cooking. He was a mystic of the kitchen, allowing the soul of a meal to emerge through his efforts.

This approach may sound passive, but, as any artist knows, it is not. The carver, the cook, the writer, the painter, the dancer, the sculptor—they all bring their creative sensibility to the process. Their own skill and passion are key ingredients in the mix. But at the same time, they all listen to the elements of their craft—to the wood or to the spices, to the words or to the paints, to the music or to the clay. And they listen to the vision that arises from both themselves and their materials and from other elements as well. They let the soul of their art flow through them, channeling their efforts and skill.

It is a co-creative process.

Parenting is the same way. For all the books and lectures and classes on how to be a good parent, much of what a mother and father must do is improvisational. Parenting takes place in the midst of the unpredictable and the unexpected. No child is ever exactly like the developmental models in the parenting courses. What works splendidly for one may not for another.

We live in a suburban neighborhood on a street that can get a fair amount of traffic coming and going in front of our house. Street safety for our kids was an early concern. John-Michael was a cautious, thoughtful child, so all Julie had to do was sit down with him on the lawn in front of the street and explain that because he was so small, the drivers in the cars going by couldn't always see him and might hit him if he went into the road. Therefore he was never to enter the street without her or me holding his hand. This explanation was all it took. We never had to worry about Johnny venturing into the street without us.

Aidan was another story. He was very focused on getting

to where he wanted to go, regardless of what was between him and his destination. (To my horror, I once saw this four-year-old charge down a store aisle to get to me, knocking aside people as he came, like a living bowling ball.) If Aidan wanted something on the other side of the street, he would simply take off after it whether or not cars were coming. No amount of explanation would change this behavior. Julie and I had to keep a sharp eye on him when he was outside, physically intervening and reprimanding him when he would head for the street. In fact, Julie had to swat his behind a couple of times before the message finally sank in. It was one of the very few times either of us has ever struck one of our kids, but Aidan was so physically motivated that only a physical shock could get through to him.

Both Aidan and Johnny stayed fairly close to home when they were small. Kaitlin, though, was our fearless adventurer. From an early age, she liked to wander off on her own. Once, when she was three, she went out the door without Julie knowing. Fortunately, one of our neighbors spotted her four blocks away from home. He was bringing her back at the same time that Julie, realizing what had happened, was heading out the door to track her down. Consequently, we always had to keep an eye on Kaitlin, too, though she was better than Aidan about not going into the street. Mostly, we didn't allow her in the front yard unattended, but she could play to her heart's content in the back, where we had a fence to corral her.

As for Maryn, she has been more like John-Michael, but then, she almost never goes anywhere without at least one sibling along, so she hasn't had the same opportunities to get into mischief.

As parents we must develop our parenting techniques in cooperation with each child. We must match the dynamic changes in our children as their personalities develop. While child development theory gives us guidelines, that is all they are; we must flesh out the details.

There is a flow about parenting that requires a flexibility, an alertness, a willingness to change and grow along with one's children. In a way, our parenting must emerge day by day, flowing from our fingers, as it were, and touching the hearts and minds of our children. In this, parenting is like any art: you let the soul of your craft and of your material act through you. In a parent's case, this is the soul of the family and of each unique child.

My father, in his cooking, was quite happy to refer to a recipe when he needed to, but he never let it limit him if he felt something greater unfolding. The soul of a child is always greater than any statistics or techniques can describe or encompass, so the soul of the parent must rise to match those potentials. It must be ready to innovate and explore to meet the child's needs.

In listening to the soul within things and acting on what she senses, a mystic uses four tools. The first is intuition, the ability to listen beyond logic and the appearance of things, to sense the subtle patterns unfolding invisibly in the world around us. It is the sixth sense. The second is inspiration, which is the willingness to be filled with a larger spirit and to be open to new perspectives that take us out of ourselves and beyond what we already know. The third is intelligence, bringing the specific knowledge and wisdom of the mind and of our experience to bear on a situation. And the fourth is improvisation, the ability to adapt, to change course, to innovate, to respond to the unique qualities of each moment, to dance with the unexpected.

These are also tools for effective and fostering parenting. They connect the interior of adult and child soul to soul, and through that connection they turn parenting into a mystical act as we discover and serve the spirit that seeks emergence.

BONES

AN IMPORTANT PART OF EMERGENCE IS THE FREEDOM we give our children to discover and to be themselves. Equally important is the structure that embraces and channels that freedom. Both children and adults need to have elements in their lives on which they can depend: the solid bones around which blood may flow, the bones that anchor the more flexible muscles.

These structures can take a variety of forms, depending on the family. Some are obvious—sitting down and eating meals together, bedtime routines, weekly religious observances, and the various traditions and rituals that families develop together. Chores and tasks can also provide structure. We have one day a week that is our major housecleaning day. Each child is assigned one or more responsibilities depending on his or her age, such as cleaning all the bathrooms or mopping the kitchen or vacuuming and dusting the living room.

One structure we have is "Kid of the Week." Each week one of our children has a turn being Kid of the Week—the person who has first choice when there is a dispute about things like which seat to have in the car, which television shows or movies to watch, who gets a window seat if we're flying in a plane, and so forth. This simple stratagem has gone a long way toward eliminating a lot of arguments. It also empowers each child, letting him or her experience added authority for a week. Generally we have found that having this authority encourages each child to be more giving and gracious to his or her siblings. Knowing he or she doesn't have to struggle or fight for a privilege allows him or her the freedom to give that privilege away or at least to share it, should that seem appropriate.

Another family structure of ours is Mental Health Day. All of our children have the right to take one day off from school per month for no other reason than that they need a day at home to play, to rest, or just to have some alone time. Julie and I have the right to veto a choice if we feel that what is going on in school that day is too important for the child to miss (no taking mental health days just to get out of a homework assignment, for example). Generally, the kids have been very responsible about the days they have chosen. Knowing that they have this option (and that they don't have to feign sickness to stay home) gives them a better attitude about going to school and has cut down on the number of spontaneous stomachaches that mysteriously arise on a school morning. It also has taught them how to gauge their feelings and not spend their mental health day carelessly but save it for when they are really needing a break.

Some families are like crystals, with highly visible and highly ordered structures and routines. The boundaries are tight. Other families are like amoebas: such a family appears to be an amorphous blob, a swirl of people going this way and that, following the currents of their particular interests, needs, and schedules, sometimes converging and sometimes not. The boundaries are loose. Both children and adults need different kinds of structures at different times in their lives, and often different children within a single family need different kinds of order and routine. Discerning and creating the kind of organization that any one person needs at a given time in her life is the challenge of parenting. That is what dancing at the edge of chaos is all about.

The metaphor of the crystal and the cell can be misleading, however, if we use it to compare levels of organization. When I was a kid, I thought of a cell as an amorphous blob with a nucleus at the center. But in college, when I took a laboratory job that entailed using an electron microscope to take pictures of protein structures within cells, I learned that the cell is really a highly organized entity with a well-defined internal "skeleton" that only looks like a blob from the outside. In effect, a cell is a living crystal, much more highly organized and complex and every bit as ordered as any diamond or piece of quartz. I realized by examining cells that the real framework of an organism is made up of patterns and flows of information. The visible structures basically facilitate the exchange and flow of information that truly does the organizing and shaping. They hold and channel energy and information so that it doesn't disperse or become lost.

A family is very much like that. A routine, such as regular family meals together, is important, not just as a repetitive action but because it provides a means for the exchange of information and presence. If we all sit around the table ignoring each other, then the routine becomes a habit that has lost its life. It has crystallized. It becomes order for order's sake. Likewise, going to a church each Sunday loses its larger meaning if it is done for social reasons or if it conveys the message that spirit is something we attend to only once a week in some special place. It is a family structure, but it may not infuse the family with a living sense of a spirit that is present everywhere, each day and in each action, and allows that the living room, kitchen, bedroom, or bathroom can also be sanctuaries.

Structure is there to enhance communication and communion, to contribute to the experience of a wholeness, to bind time and space so that they can hold the energy and information and, most important, the love that is the living tissue of a healthy family. The bones in our bodies give us rigidity and form, but they also produce the blood that circulates and brings life to the whole. The bones of our families do not have to be hard, crystalline routines, either, there just to give shape to our days and form to our years. They are there to produce the family blood of love and nourishment.

For example, I do not let a day go by without telling each of my children how proud I am of them just for being who they are.

I do not let a day go by without hugging them and telling them I love them.

I do not let a day go by without making them laugh or singing a song to them.

I do not let a day go by without expressing interest in

what they are doing and asking them to share with me what has happened in their day.

I do not let a day go by without praising them at least once about something they have done.

These are simple things, not visible to an outsider looking for the routines that shape the life of our family. But they are every bit as much a structure as having dinner together every day; they are means through which the love that is the life and soul of the family circulates. They are family bones.

There are other structures, too, that are invisible but vastly important to the shape and balance of a family. These are the values we inhabit and express—our beliefs, our attitudes, our virtues. These are the bones of courage, kindness, humor, responsibility, compassion, and self-worth that give our lives form. These qualities can be hard as granite, solid foundations on which to build character and through which to channel spirit and action.

The family is the place where the bones of character are made—but not simply through instruction. They are formed by example. Like a transplant, they pass from parent to child. They can also pass in the opposite direction, for children can offer in return their openness and wonderment, a life-embracing innocence, even courage and faith. In a family, we are bone-makers for each other.

My son John-Michael comes to mind. Reading and writing did not come easily to John-Michael. He required special tutoring, but even then, he was always behind many others in his class. Although the schools he attended avoided comparisons and competition between students and allowed each child to progress at his or her own pace, Johnny could not help but see that in these areas he was not matching his friends' abilities. I worried about what he might be feeling. So one afternoon, when he was twelve, I talked with him about it. "Well, Dad," he said, "I know many of my friends are ahead of me in reading, but that's all right. We each have our different skills. I feel good about myself and what I *can* do. That's what's important to me. I can always catch up with my reading."

John-Michael's self-esteem was a revelation to me. When I was that age, I was always concerned about what others thought of me and wanted to do well to gain their approval. It was a constant pressure. But Johnny felt none of that. He felt graceful about who he was and what he could do, and he did not begrudge others their success. (Indeed, he has outstanding people skills and was recently given a citation for his work as a conflict mediator in his school by a special four-city task force honoring local youths and their contributions to their communities.)

As someone who still struggles at times with issues of self-esteem and the need to prove myself, I found his sense of self-worth and his insightful perspective on his abilities and challenges a lesson and an inspiration, a bone that could help me in my own inner life.

In this context, most important to the structure of a family is the character of the people who make it up. Families reflect who we are; they manifest how we deal with relationships, with communication, and with feelings, responsibility, and spirit. Families are the externalization of our presence. And it is our presence—the very field of our beings, the energy of who we are—that ultimately organizes and shapes the character and quality of the family, whatever the outer routines may be.

We are not just bone-makers, we are the bones—flexible bones of information and spirit, energy and life.

Which takes us into the domain of the mystic. It might be thought that a mystic is someone whose path moves away from structure and bone, flesh and form, to diffuse into a transcendent unity. In my experience, though, this would be incorrect. The task I feel as a mystic is not just to connect with the sacred, but to understand how it manifests within the organization of the universe. What are the bones of the sacred? What are the ways in which information and spirit, energy and life are generated and transmitted throughout creation?

At the heart of many of my mystical experiences over the

years is the perception that creation itself is a family; we are all relations, as the Native Americans put it. We are kin to the stars and atoms, born from each; we are cousins to trees and meadows, rocks and rivers, spiders and foxes, ravens and bears, salmon and whales, and all the grand symphony of life visible and invisible, known and unknown, that fills the universe. And as in any family, it is ultimately who we are, the quality of our presence, that provides the bones great and small that shape the whole.

Creating family, nourishing family, being the bones of family: that is part of what a mystic does. For family is also the context for emergence, the womb from which new possibilities and potentials arise and take on, in part at least, the shape of the bones that support that womb. So how these bones are formed is important. The understanding of bones—of structure—is as important on the mystical path as the understanding of spirit.

We are all building bones all the time. What the mystic brings to this is a recognition of the spirit that lights that process, and an understanding that the function of bones is to serve that spirit. Jesus said the same when he pointed out that the Sabbath was made for man, not man for the Sabbath. The bone was made for the unfoldment of spirit, not the other way around.

So the mystic looks beyond structure and form to see the

spirit, the essence, the presence that seek expression in the moment. The mystic asks if the bone that is there is appropriate to the life that seeks to emerge. Does it serve the circulation of the sacred?

Thus, when parents do more than inherit the bones of their upbringing, the routines and images of their past, and use them simply because they are familiar—when they look to see what routines, what structures, what bones truly serve their children and the soul that seeks emergence in their family—they are performing a mystical act.

GHOSTS

SOMETIMES I FEEL THAT FAMILY LIFE IS NOT UNLIKE walking through a haunted house on one of those dark, spooky nights when a cloud-shrouded moon tries to avert its gaze and a mournful wind moans and whispers at the eaves. You never know just what is going to jump out at you.

One afternoon, I was trying to get Kaitlin, who was three or four at the time, ready to meet Julie and the two boys for dinner. My daughter, however, was not cooperating. She was in play mode, running around, hiding from me, giggling and laughing, generally having a great time. At first I got into the spirit of it, trying to entice her playfully into changing her clothes and putting on her shoes. But as the game (to her) went on, I became more and more frustrated and aware of how little time we had. Finally, I managed to get her into her shoes and a clean dress, but as I turned away to get her jacket, I heard a thump behind me. Turning back, I discovered she had playfully hurled one shoe across the room and was in the process of taking the other one off, giggling all the while.

At this point, I lost it in a way I have rarely experienced. I had stumbled into a dark corridor within myself, and to my astonishment a ghost had lurched out and seized me by the throat. I found myself consumed by an anger as intense as any I had ever felt. I just wanted to scream and hit something (an ancient mystical technique for discharging unwanted energy). At that moment, I knew that what I most wanted to hit was Kaitlin, the source of my frustration. At that moment, I was one with every parent who has ever come to the end of his or her rope, felt it snap, and proceeded to bash their child against a wall.

I couldn't do that. To commit any kind of violence against a child is, to me, the lowest thing that any human being can do. Even in the extremity of my rage, I knew I could not and would not hit my daughter. If part of me knew in that moment the horror of a parent who loses control, I also felt the strength of the vast majority of parents who, reaching a similar point of anger, hang on to their sanity and refuse to become violent. But as I stood there, trembling with this energy, I knew I had to do something to release it. So I screamed and kicked at a large pillow that was lying on the floor. Unfortunately, I missed, hit a footstool instead, and broke my big toe! At which point, as I hopped about on one foot, holding my throbbing toe, my anger was replaced by such a feeling of humor that I ended up on the floor laughing. Kaitlin, thoroughly startled by what had just happened, suddenly put her shoes back on and, taking her crazy Daddy by the hand, led us both out the door to meet Julie and her brothers.

When one steps onto the mystical path, the expectation may be of a journey through realms of light and love and peacefulness. The truth is far different. The challenge for a mystic is not only to discover oneness with the sacred but also with himself. This means deliberately walking into those dark and shadowy places within, where fears lurk and repressed images wait to reveal themselves. And if we don't know how to engage those shadows, the invocation of spiritual energy into our lives will almost certainly bring them to the surface—sometimes when we least expect it.

When one has a spiritual teacher or mentor, it is often the task of that person to bring these unresolved fragments of self and soul to one's attention. Lacking that, I have discovered that children will do the job just as well, if not better. I challenge any abbot or guru to probe as deeply, unlock as many weaknesses, and press as many buttons as a child can do by being himself.

For me, one of those unresolved fragments was my anger. I am by nature a tolerant and patient fellow; it takes a lot to get me angry. What I didn't realize, though, was how often I would store unresolved feelings like kindling. When the spark came that finally set me ablaze, I would discover myself in the midst of a bonfire. Oh, it would burn out quickly; I don't stay angry for very long, and I don't carry grudges. Once the fire's out, it's out. But in the moment, it would be far too intense for my liking.

I had rarely been in a situation to confront this aspect of myself until I had children. Then I began to discover just how angry I could get, for each of my kids has a way of getting inside me and liberating my inner ghosts.

In part, this is because they mirror me so well. When they reflect back some part of me that I am proud of, then I am happy. But when they show me something that I struggle with or don't like in myself, well, then I can get angry. The anger is not so much at them but at having that trait or condition brought back into my life to deal with, which is usually a good indication that I am not finished dealing with it myself.

For example, I have always struggled with a stubborn streak in my nature that can make me uncooperative and moody. At times, I am happy for this trait, for there are situations when being stubborn serves a good purpose. But, at other times, it separates me from people and turns me into a curmudgeon. It can become a source of rigidity that I don't appreciate in myself.

Unfortunately, in recent years, I have seen Kaitlin exhibiting the same stubbornness, which sometimes gets turned against her siblings for no good reason (just as mine would have, I'm sure, if I had had brothers or sisters!). When this trait comes out in her, it makes me angry primarily because it puts me in touch with my own struggles. It lets me know that I have not resolved this particular ghost in my life.

By the same token, my children can offer me ways of exorcising these ghosts, not by expressing them necessarily but by understanding them. I'm sure I will finally come to terms with my own stubborn moods not by reacting to their reflection in Kaitlin but by helping her deal with them in her own life. Likewise, I can learn from the strategies that she develops.

For example, around the age of six or so, Kaitlin realized that she was subject to moods, and when she was feeling out of sorts, she would go off on her own to let the energy settle so she could change it. I have seen her be in the foulest of bad moods, angry and yelling at everyone, but then, before Julie or I could intervene, go back to her room and close the door. She'd sit in silence for a while, and then come back out fifteen or twenty minutes later, her inner storm passed, cooperative, smiling, and friendly again. She knew exactly what she needed to do to quiet her energy, and she would do it.

I learned a lot just watching her do this.

Aidan is the opposite of Kaitlin in this respect. Whereas Kaitlin can be very up front about what she is feeling, carrying her mood around like a flashing neon sign, Aidan is very private about his emotions, and sometimes he doesn't know himself just what he's feeling. In terms of how he handles his moods, Aidan is also a lot like me. I have always been a very private person, reticent about sharing my feelings with others. But this reticence is also how I pick up and store the emotional kindling for my bonfires of anger.

Julie and I have worked hard with Aidan to give him tools to name and express his feelings appropriately. His tendency as a child was to translate a feeling directly into an action, like hitting someone. So it was with pleasure and astonishment that I watched him one day when he was about ten years old. I was driving all the kids into town to do some shopping at the local mall. As we rode in the car, he turned to his siblings and said clearly and distinctly, "I am feeling very out of sorts right now and angry, and it would be help-ful to me if you didn't talk to me for a while or joke with me. I know if you do, I'll get angry and I might hit you, and I don't want to do that!"

This was an amazing thing for Aidan to say, and it repre-sented a real breakthrough for him. He brought one of his ghosts right out into the open and said, in effect, "Here it is, everybody. Help me with it." Since then he has learned to do this more regularly and has become very articulate about his feelings when the need arises. But the incident was also a great encouragement for me because I knew that if Aidan could be so open, I could, too. And since then, I *have* been much more open myself, sharing what I'm feeling, and get-ting rid of the kindling before it self-combusts.

In both these cases, I have learned from my children how to get out my own ghosts; my children were parenting me.

One of the problems in dealing with anger and other negative or hurtful emotions or thoughts is that we judge ourselves. We feel bad for having them. I have found this es-pecially true for people on a spiritual path. But we need to accept that our families, filled with people whom we love and care for and who love and care for us, can stimulate these hidden emotions like no one else, and to understand that this process is natural and part of the growth of all concerned.

It has been my experience on the mystical path that the response of spirit to negativity is not to judge it or condemn it but to release the energy contained within it—in effect, to exorcise it. So Julie and I seek to do this with the ghosts we find in our family closets.

The first and most important step is to create a safe environment for all of us. I know of no substitute for this. A safe environment is one in which a person can bring forth her haunts without fear of judgment or blame.

For example, one evening while I was back in the bedroom, I heard a cry from the living room and ran out to see what had happened. It turned out that Aidan, who was three at the time, had marched out of the kitchen where he had been having an argument with his mother. He had come up beside John-Michael who was sitting on the couch peacefully watching a cartoon on the television and, without any preamble or warning, had slugged him. When we asked Aidan why he had done that, he said that he was angry at Mommy, but he couldn't hit her, so he hit Johnny instead.

Now, this is a perfectly understandable situation. It's scary to be angry at Mommy or Daddy when you're a child. There is an immense power differential between an adult and a child based on age, size, strength, and experience. Part of creating safety for a child is letting him know that a parent will not use his power advantage in an unfair or hurtful way.

So we have always let our kids know that it is all right to feel anger at us, that it is not a sign of disrespect nor will it cost them our love. The anger is not the issue; what is important is how they express their anger. We have let them know that there are appropriate ways, such as words, and inappropriate ways, such as hitting.

Similarly, I used to feel that it would be wrong for me to bring an energy like anger into the family setting, because I wanted that to be a place of safety and peace. But, of course, everyone knew when I was angry anyway, and after I exploded a few times, the kids and Julie let me know they would rather I tell them when I was angry instead of letting it build. This was very liberating, because they were extending safety to me to express my feelings.

But the real safety comes from knowing that you can liberate a ghost and not be possessed by it. Knowing that I had not harmed Kaitlin that day when I exploded gave me great confidence in expressing my anger at other times because I knew I could trust myself; I knew I was safe. In the years since, the increase in my ability to experience and express anger easily and even gently has been a revelation. It was my family who created a safe place where I could learn that, just as I seek to create a safe place for them to learn their lessons.

The second step in an inner exorcism is to name the ghost. Sometimes it is anger, sometimes it is fear, sometimes it is something else. Sometimes it is nothing: only an echo, a shadow that fades as soon as light hits it. But being able to name it, discuss it, bring it into the light of day, is powerfully healing and helps release the embarrassment and tension that otherwise bind it to us. It's good to know that whatever the haunting feeling may be, having it is not the end of the world. You will not be banished from the family.

Children need to learn how to name their feelings and to know that simply by naming a feeling, they take away its power to control them. Rather than rant and rave around the house, Kaitlin or Aidan can say very clearly, "I am feeling frustrated now," or sad, or whatever it might be, and that feeling will be heard and respected.

The final step is to release the energy of the ghost. Sometimes, just listening to a person say what she is feeling or naming the emotion or thought is enough. Other times, we might need to get at the energy in innovative ways. How might the anger or fear or grief be expressed in a different way? Maybe we can dance it away. Maybe we can turn it into music. Maybe we can run with it. Maybe we need to hug each other or form laps; maybe we need to play a game or watch a movie. Or maybe we just need to have some silence.

In everyday life, we can find different strategies for not exploring our shadowy places, and sometimes we can get away with it for quite a while. But once you step onto a mystical path or a parental one, it is only a matter of time before the ghosts come out. But the power of a family, as well as the power of spirit, to create a safe, loving, and transformative environment can never be overestimated. If we can take what jumps out at us in the humor and light of such an environment, we can discover that most ghosts are only as powerful as the shadows in which they were hidden.

WOUNDS

When John-Michael was two and Julie was pregnant with Aidan, we decided to go to Disneyland, knowing that after Aidan was born it would be at least another two years before we could make the trip. The first day was an unending routine of standing under a hot sun in one infinite line after another (even the rides began to seem like lines), and when evening came around, we were all tired. We decided to treat ourselves to a good meal in one of the Disneyland Hotel's restaurants. So after dressing up, we presented ourselves to the hostess and asked for a table for three.

I was, by then, experienced enough in the ways of John-Michael and restaurants to hope we would get a quiet booth somewhere off in a shadowy corner. Unfortunately, the only table available was a round one right in the middle of everything and everyone. If there had been a spotlight in the ceiling, we would have been center stage. "And now," I could imagine the announcer saying, "we present, The Spanglers At Dinner! Featuring, The Tired Child!"

It was, truly, the dinner from hell. The restaurant was crowded and the service was oh, so slow, leading me to suspect that Sleepy and Dopey were doing the cooking John Michael was so tired that somewhere between the soup and salad, he finally just lost it. Like a damned soul from a Night on Bald Mountain, he screamed. He fussed. He cried. He knocked over his water glass. I cringed. Julie handled it with her usual calmness and aplomb, but eventually it was more than even her soothing presence could handle.

Finally, the main course arrived, which calmed Johnny down enough for him to take a bite or two, at which point he began crying again (I actually thought the food was rather good, but then you already know about my sense of taste). Nor was crying sufficient. Food began flying as my son sought to remove the offending morsels from his plate. The rubble of a once fine dinner piled up on the floor around us like the remains of a World War II artillery barrage. Finally, Julie snatched him up, said, "Finish your dinner. I'll see you later!" and headed off to the hotel room.

In the shocked silence that descended on the dining room as she left, I sat there in the middle of everything, debris all around me, trying to pretend that nothing was out of the ordinary as I "finished my dinner." Just then, the hostess brought by a very well-dressed and elegant couple on their way to a vacant table. As they went by, it was like a glacier passing, cold and unforgiving. Behind my back, I heard the lady say, "My God, pigs must have eaten there!" At which point, having more than reached my maximum level of humiliation, I arose and fled from the scene.

Having humbling experiences is traditionally considered good form on the mystical path. Such experiences are seen as keeping the ego in line, wounding the pride that would separate us from the sacred. Of course, a night of humiliation over a messy dinner makes for a funny story, the kind of thing it's nice to open a chapter with, but as a wound, it hardly qualifies as a scratch on the psyche of any mystic worth his prayer beads. Within minutes of leaving the restaurant, it simply became something to laugh about, another episode in the continuing initiation into the joys and perils of fatherhood.

In the Western spiritual tradition, wounds and wounded-ness often occupy a special position as signs of faith and virtue. I remember traveling to Assisi once, the home of St. Francis, and viewing the hair shirt he wore (with patches of dried blood still visible) and the small whip with which he flagellated himself in an attempt to purify his soul. It was a reminder of the particular kind of religious sensibility that sees the path to God as a path of suffering and pain.

But wounds are not the special property of saints and holy men; they are the lot of all of us. In particular, when we be-come parents and children enter our lives, all our carefully designed controls and defenses begin to go out the window, and we realise just how vulnerable we can be. And when we become vulnerable, we can become wounded.

The job of a parent is one of the toughest in the world. It is filled with challenges made all the more challenging be-cause we are emotionally involved. We are in love and vul-nerable. The fact that we want to do so much for our children, and end up at times feeling we can only do so little, can be wounding.

When John-Michael was sick for no reason the doctor could understand and just lay on the couch for days listless and feverish, I felt wounded.

When I have seen my child struggling to read and write

because the part of his brain that processes language just doesn't work the way it does in the average person, I have felt wounded.

When my finances have been dicey and I've wondered whether I can earn enough to support my family, I have felt wounded.

When I want to be with my kids but my work takes me away from them, I have felt wounded.

Knowing that in my most angry and frustrated moments I can have feelings of violence toward my kids fills me with shame. Never mind that almost all parents feel such things from time to time, the fact that I feel them makes me feel wounded.

When I look out at a society that poisons its air, its water, and its food, that encourages kids to live on sugar, that sells them violence as entertainment or deliberately targets them as tobacco consumers and drug users, that wastes their imaginations and intelligence, that seeks to straitjacket them into conformity to the past, that either glorifies or demeans them but doesn't treat them as the growing people they are, and that allows conditions to exist where children go to bed hungry, abused, or frightened, then I feel wounded—not just on my own children's behalf, but on behalf of children everywhere.

When I see a society that would rob Kaitlin and Maryn of

their voices, take away their strength, and confine them to accepted roles of "femininity," or that would shape Johnny and Aidan into molds of aggressive and unfeeling "masculinity," I feel wounded.

Most parents I know share these kinds of wounds. Many have much worse ones, such as the trauma of divorce or the death of a child. If you are at all caring and fostering, wounds come with the territory. You cannot love your children without becoming vulnerable to all the dangers that can beset them and the ignorance and stereotyping that can diminish them. Parenting can be a walk in the park, but it can also be a walk into a combat zone with your loved ones.

The challenge comes not from our capacity to be wounded but in how we deal with our wounds. Like her siblings before her when they were younger, my three-year-old, Maryn, will sometimes come to sit on my lap and point out all the small "owies" on her body. "Look, Daddy, here's an owie and here's an owie, and there's an owie, and . . ." She is not actually in pain, but she wants my sympathy. Sometimes it is a way of trying to manipulate me into doing something for her—as in, "Daddy, I have an owie. Can I watch a movie on TV?" But sometimes it is a recounting of her body's history, a way of making a statement about who she is and what she has experienced. Her owies become embodied memories around which she fashions her identity in that moment.

We can see the same behavior in society as people present their owies to each other for sympathy and commiseration, to manipulate and control, or to establish who they are. My friend Carolyn Myss calls this phenomenon woundology, and she says that people don't heal because their wounds are too important to them to let go. Unlike Maryn and other young children who can identify with their owies in one moment and then move on to identify with something else in the next, adults can become stuck in their woundedness. The wounds become a means of seeking some kind of social standing, a basis for communication, a badge of identity.

If I am stuck in my wounds, however, I can project my woundedness into my relationships, allowing them to color my expectations and my behavior. At the least, this can add a sad, bitter, or disempowered tinge to my life. At worst it becomes toxic, an excuse to inflict wounds on others.

From a mystical perspective, I believe that wounds need not be glorified, nor are they necessary as a means of spiritual development. But when they occur, they must be embraced and their pain accepted so that we can move on. To either cling to my wounds or to deny them is to keep them open and suppurating. But acceptance is not enough. For healing and closure to occur, there must be forgiveness.

After the novel *Love Story* came out, it became quite popular to say, "Love means never having to say you're sorry."

This sounds nice, but it's poor human relations and poor mysticism. The act of contrition, of saying, "I'm sorry. I apologize," can be very important, particularly in opening the door to forgiveness. While it is true that where there is love there can be automatic forgiveness, not taking this for granted, bringing the process of making amends into the open, can lead to powerful healing.

Parents know how important saying "I'm sorry" can be in resolving disputes between children. For a while, it seemed that Julie and I were forever asking one of our children to apologize to another for this or that. The fact was that without a simple statement that acknowledged responsibility, or at least participation in whatever caused the other upset, the conflict wasn't resolved. It just smoldered.

Parents also must know how to ask for their children's forgiveness and, if necessary, make amends. The only way Julie or I can really teach our children the power of an apology is to apologize ourselves when we have acted wrongly or thoughtlessly. And the only way we can teach forgiveness is to forgive.

As a parent, I must accept that I am vulnerable to pain— the pain of feeling powerless at times, or scared, or humiliated, or angry, or any of the other emotions that can spring out like ghosts from the shadowy places inside. I feel pain over not being perfect all the time, the ideal dad. But it is especially important for us as parents to forgive the condition of parenthood for being a source of pain and to forgive ourselves for our perceived or imagined failings. If amends or changes are truly necessary, we cannot move forward until we have released our guilt and anger toward ourselves. It is inevitable that as parents we will make mistakes; hopefully they will be small ones and not the kinds that drive children to the hospital, or the psychiatrist, or even to prisons. Mistakes notwithstanding, we must transform our image that parents have to be perfect or that parents can do no wrong. We must accept ourselves as ordinary human beings, and as extraordinary souls. Only then can we begin to heal or forgive.

In this context, there is a need for parents to be warriors and to courageously face what may appear to be dark truths about themselves. Sometimes parents need to be warriors anyway just to get up in the morning—to face all the hassles and stresses of daily life, to make a decent and healthy life for their children. To face one's inner shadows, one's wounds, and to begin to heal and forgive can take real courage.

This is especially true if a person comes from a toxic family, one where abuse has been prevalent, for example. To stand in the presence of pain from such a past and say, "It stops here. I will not pass this on to my children," is the act of a warrior, an act of profound courage—particularly since one of the ways we release the pain and tension of our own demons is to pass that energy on to others. To refuse to do so is to risk that the pain will stay with you. But by gathering and holding that pain and not inflicting it on others, you take a step toward your healing and its dissipation.

Here is where a spiritual perspective and practice can truly help. If a mystic gains anything in contemplating the sacred, it is the knowledge of a love within creation that can embrace any shadow and bring it to light, take on any wound and bring it to healing. When dealing with our own wounds and the tenderness of our vulnerabilities, expressing that love with each other and with our children can be a true gift of grace.

TIME

WITH EACH OF MY CHILDREN, THERE HAS COME A TIME when they have wanted their own watch. Each time, Julie or I have said, "When you can tell time, then you can have a watch." At which point the conversation goes something like this:

"I don't want a face watch. I want one of those watches with numbers. Then I can tell time by reading the numbers."

"Do you know what the numbers mean?"

"Sure. They're the time!"

For our children, time is a mysterious and wonderful thing, and wearing a watch, especially one that reduces time to numbers, seems to offer a way of controlling it, or at least touching its magic. But it is not only children who are fascinated by it. We are all engaged by the mystery of time, and in a mystical sense, in the mystery of timelessness.

When I am meditating, time falls away. Past, present, and future converge and collapse into a state of timeless being. In fact, once at a conference, I was asked to lead a meditation for several hundred people. It was to be a short interlude of quiet before the lunch break. It started out well; I had everyone close their eyes for a very brief visualization, followed by silence. But when I opened my eyes, thinking only five minutes or so had gone by, the auditorium was almost entirely empty. To my chagrin, I had lost track of time and had been sitting there for almost forty minutes. Most of the audience had simply gotten up quietly and gone off to lunch, probably figuring I had gone to sleep. Such are the perils of timelessness. You wouldn't want to set your watch by it, with or without numbers.

As a parent, I experience timelessness as well, only in that case it is the "lessness" of time. There simply is never enough of it. As the number of our children has grown, the rate at which time disappears has increased. Perhaps through parenting, I have stumbled on the secret to becoming one with the eternal: have more children!

Though physicists have gained deeper and deeper insights into time as a dimension of existence in the physical universe, it still retains an elusive quality. For one thing, it's highly subjective. We don't all experience time in the same way. Five minutes can go by like the wind for one person and drag on for days for another. Ask any child sitting at the dinner table waiting for his parents to finish their meals before he can be excused.

When I teach my children to "tell time," on the surface I am teaching them to decipher the meaning of a clock or a calendar, both of which are purely human constructs. But I am also teaching them how to enter their imaginations and how to deal with the realm of abstractions, things invisible to the senses but real to the mind. It is in that realm that a child begins to learn about consequences and connections. With an understanding of time, I can say to Kaitlin, for example, "If you take your mental health day today, the consequence will be that you will not be able to take it next week and stay home when your brother is having his birthday." And she will understand and be able to make the choice she wishes.

In the abstract realm to which time gives access, I have a wider view of patterns of connection and consequences. I can see that if I want money for college ten years down the line, I must start saving now. And in John-Michael, for example, I can see an interest in and an ability with mechanical things that is like that of his paternal great-grandfather. I see him in the wider context of family history. In the context of understanding time, I and my children can discover a larger sense of self, one that extends into the past and the future.

Teaching our children about time is a gift of imagination that opens them to multiple possibilities for growth, development, and play. But time is also another kind of gift, the gift of ourselves. Time is also a way of describing our availability and accessibility: the capacity of being there for our children. All parents know this is important. And in our society, all parents know how difficult it can be, especially when economic conditions seem to make it necessary in most families for both parents to work.

It is equally important, if the family is to be healthy and the bones of the family strong, that parents have time to not be parents as well. Children may take everything you have to offer, but you need to know how much you can give and still maintain balance. A burned-out parent is no help to his children. The soul that lives within each parent is more than just a parent and needs opportunities, just like children, to discover and express other dimensions of personality. Parents are "selfing," too.

For example, Julie attends a regular drumming class and has a women's group. She and I also try to get out together regularly (much easier now that Johnny and Aidan are both old enough to baby-sit—and do an excellent job of it!).

Still, when a couple becomes parents, they are taking on a special commitment and making a sacrifice. And the most important sacrifice they make is their time. Both my mystical and personal experiences convince me how important this is to the parenting process. Children are not just there as accessories while parents go on about their own lives as if they were just a couple. Parents do need to be nurtured and to nurture themselves, but when they became parents, they lost some of their privileges to make those needs a priority. When it comes down to it, the child's needs are paramount, especially when he is still young (teenagers often don't want their parents around anyway, though that doesn't mean they don't still need them).

Sacrifice has always played a role in the spiritual paths of the world. The simple truth is, to gain something larger, you have to let go of something smaller. To enjoy the richness that a family can offer, the power of love that a family can invoke when all its members are pulling together—being bone and blood together—means that I have to surrender some of the patterns and habits I had when I was single. Just as to experience the rich complexity of the soul, I will have to surrender some of the simplistic and limited perspectives and habits of the personality.

Both mysticism and parenting are paths of sacrifice; it's just that sometimes, parents don't want to admit it.

Which brings us back to time. The idea that all a parent need do is spend "quality" time with a child has been disproved in recent childhood and family studies that I have seen. That is not surprising. Not that putting quality into one's interaction with a child is not important and good, but who is defining quality? The parent? The child? To a parent, quality time in the midst of a busy schedule may mean intense and focused time, like a laser burst of attentiveness. But living things do not grow well under lasers. They require a more relaxed time for the complex bondings to take place. Think of sunlight that is always present.

In fact, this kind of relaxed time can occur even when a parent is not paying direct attention. There are times when I am working in my office and one of my children will come in and just sit with me or play on the floor near me. My daughter Kaitlin did that this morning as I was writing this book. She knew I did not want to be disturbed, but she sat in a chair behind me, looking out the window and reading a book. I enjoyed her presence, and she enjoyed mine. It was no great effort to smile at her occasionally or to extend my sense of presence to include her. I still got my work done. We were exchanging sunlight together.

If I make time my enemy, then I am always fighting it.

Even when I have time with my kids, I may be thinking of it in a context of the time that I don't have. I may even be regretting the time that I don't have for something else. After all, let's face it, with all the love in the world, spending time with children is not always the most stimulating and exciting thing an adult can do. And that's nobody's fault. Kids sometimes find each other boring, too. And heaven knows that there are times I find other adults boring (but then, I'm usually feeling boring myself at such moments, so who knows what I'm inflicting on them).

If I don't think about the time but instead think about being available, about extending my presence, about just being together and being sunlight, it takes some of the pressure off. I'm not trying for "quality time" but just to be present in the moment. When I am with my children, I don't think about it as "spending time with them" but simply as being with them, whatever occurs.

And if when I am not with them, I can still hold them in my sense of presence (for to my soul there is no distance between us), then I am still being sunshine. They will feel it.

Still, it is true that the more time I have available, the more availability I can provide, the better it is for my child (and me). It is breadth, not narrow focus, that provides the best context for growth and nourishment. So it may well be that a family sometimes needs to reexamine its priorities, its criteria for success, and its needs and desires, and prioritize in ways that will make more availability possible. As part of that evaluation, it is important to determine just what availability means, for it is defined by more than time. It is also determined by the presence of heart and soul. Creating a schedule to spend one hour more a week or twenty minutes more a day with a child is not the same as creating more availability (though it may certainly be a start). Availability is a state of mind apart from time, a willingness to be open and to be present, without expectation, without condition, without qualification, solely because you love.

Like God, it is, in effect, timeless.

Spirituality

We were performing a simple ritual in the living room. I forget now what the occasion was, but we were invoking blessings on the family and on our world. I had lit a candle in the center of the room to represent the one Light that fills and surrounds us all. As we sat around it, I asked each family member to say something like, "I invoke the presence of love," or "I invoke the presence of peace for the world." We went around the circle in this way until we came to Maryn, who was sitting in Julie's lap (she was two at the time). She looked around at all of us, gave us one of her patented dimpled smiles, and said, "I . . ." and she stumbled over the word *invoke,* "I . . . want presents, too. A necklace and a Barbie. Please!"

Such is spiritual life in the Spangler household.

Where the mystical dimension and the everyday world of the family usually intersect most overtly is in the spirituality that the family practices. As far as mysticism is concerned, there are many different ways to go. I have friends whose spiritual practices range from Tibetan Buddhism to A Course in Miracles, from Catholicism to Druidry, from New Age to Zen, and from Paganism to Protestantism.

There are those who say that religion is the enemy of spirituality, but I do not agree with that. Certainly, a case can be made that religious organizations can be intolerant and conservative (but then, a tradition is supposed to be conservative in the sense of conserving or saving for future generations the wisdom and insights of those who have gone before). In the midst of dogma and ritual, people can sometimes lose the living spirit that gave birth to the religion in the first place. But there are many examples of how traditional practices have provided touchstones with the sacred, and of how individuals in religious organizations have transcended doctrinal

differences to offer unconditional compassion and service to
the world. It is people who make a particular religious tradition open or closed, vibrant or stultified, a foundation for
freedom or a box for tyranny. If one decries the arrogance
and blindness of a church's claim that God can only be found
within its walls, it makes no sense either to say that God and
spirit can only be found outside them. God goes where she
will, and visits the hearts of the tolerant and the intolerant,
those who include and those who exclude, the expansive and
the limited.

I would agree, though, that spirituality is not the same as
religion, the former being in my mind a larger category. I
would see religion as a particular manifestation of a greater
spiritual impulse. But I would equally acknowledge that in
the proper hands and with the proper vision, business, science, art, sports, or even politics can also be vehicles for
spiritual expression. The fact that they do not use the language of spirituality or religion does not alter in the least the
potential of spirit to flow in and through them.

In this regard, building a family can certainly be a spiritual
practice.

The form of spirituality that a family practices—the beliefs, rituals, celebrations, and traditions that it incorpo-
rates—is part of the uniqueness of that family. If it is going
to serve the family (and remember that Jesus said religious

observations like the Sabbath were meant to serve people, not the other way around), there needs to be a resonance with the souls of that family and its members. What works well for one may not work for another.

Perhaps one reason religion and spirituality are often seen as opposites is that families tend to inherit their religion, whether it truly touches the soul of the family or not. So they end up with a practice that exists as a form for them to follow but is not necessarily a dynamic connection with the sacred in their lives. People tend to blame the religion rather than to realize that they have not investigated it or themselves deeply enough to see if and where a connection can be made.

Over the years I have met a great many people who, after many years of seeking and trying different spiritual paths, end up back in the religion of their forebears—but with a deeper connection to its spirit because of their other experiences. And there are others who never go back but find in another tradition or in an eclectic spirituality the resonance they were seeking.

Because I feel each family must find its own spiritual identity, I am certainly not going to prescribe one. But I will offer some thoughts about spirituality and some specific images from my own path.

One of the functions that I feel spirituality should perform is to help an individual find his or her power and speak in his or her authentic voice. After all, spirituality is about connection with the sacred, which manifests uniquely in each individual. In the Western tradition (especially in America), we pride ourselves on supporting individuality and recognizing the sovereign rights and privileges of the individual. In fact, though, much of what goes on in society—in education, religion, politics, and business—pressures us to conform or to act as a mass. A true expression of individuality is often a little frightening, for every individual is a slice of Mystery to everyone else. So let's diminish the fear here and get everyone more or less practicing the same lifestyle, sharing the same values, believing in the same things, and buying the same products. Let's be one big happy tribe that has eliminated any taint of otherness!

This goes against the natural grain of spirit. From a mystic's point of view, there is room for everyone, however eccentric, in the body of God. The co-creative power of the sacred is best expressed not in sameness but where differences meet. So, for me, a spirituality should honor difference and support the discovery of a person's deepest voice, the one closest to her soul's intent, even when it is different from the voice of her family.

In the movie *Hook,* Peter Pan—having grown up, gotten married, had children, and, in the process, forgotten who he really is—is trying to save his kidnapped son and daughter from Captain Hook and his pirates. However, because he has forgotten his magical nature, he has no power with which to fight Hook. In the climactic scene, Peter remembers that to be the Pan and regain his powers, he must remember his happy thought, the one thought that will restore his magic. As he thinks about this, he realizes that his happy thought was about being a father, about holding his newborn son and daughter in his arms. That was his happy thought, and when he remembered it, he could fly, he could crow, and he could fight, and he rescued his children. (I cried when I saw that, for being a father was and is my happy thought, too. Though it doesn't seem to enable me to fly.)

Spirituality should reveal our "happy thought" to us: the vision or presence at our core that blesses us and gives us the power to be ourselves in the midst of a world that wishes us all too often to be someone or something else.

Spirituality should open us to the sacrament of the ordinary and the holiness of everyday objects and events. In a workshop I once illustrated this by asking the participants to bring things from their home or work with which to build an altar. I started things off by bringing a toaster (after all, it can provide burnt offerings). It was a revelation to many of them that an altar didn't have to have crosses or flowers or pictures of gurus or crystals or any religious icons at all in order to be a place for invoking the sacred. It enabled them to go back to their houses and offices and see altars and places of magic where before they had only seen obstructions and distractions.

Not just ordinary things but ordinary actions can be sacramental. In our family, we stress the "please"s and "thank you"s and other little acts of mutual respect and courtesy not only because they are good manners but also because they bring grace into human relations. Being courteous is also to my mind a little appreciated but powerful act of magic. For example, I went to the neighborhood Blockbuster a while ago to check out a video for the evening. Approaching the door, I was preceded by a young couple dressed in leather, their hair spiked and colored, and their bodies pierced in an amazing variety of places. You could have knocked me over with a feather when the young man opened the door for me and courteously stood to one side, saying, "After you, sir." It was a simple act, made more remarkable and vibrant for me by shattering my images about "punk people," but it certainly raised my energy level and sent me home on a wave of good feeling. Could there be a better magic than that? I was transformed.

For me, the practice of spirituality is very much about such energy, and how to work creatively with it. I am sensitive to the energies that people and places emit, and, because of this, I know only too well the power of moods to affect our environments and each other. Kaitlin definitely felt the energy that was pouring from me the day I got mad at her and broke my toe. I did not have to strike her physically to have an effect.

One of the responsibilities that comes with the mystical path is being aware of one's moods and the energy one puts out; that responsibility and the self-reflection that it requires is part of my spirituality, but it can be part of anyone's. This is not an esoteric thing. We are all aware of how our moods can affect others; it's just that too often we don't do much about it. But we can do damage to our children by making them the targets of our angry or depressed feelings whether or not we act them out.

With respect to spirituality, our children learn about the sacred and the values of love, compassion, and wholeness not through things Julie and I teach them but from watching us in action. We make our spirituality very much part of our family, conveying our conviction that everything we do with and to each other is a spiritual act. Our children's need is to connect fully and in a healthy way with the earth and the people around them and to have a spiritual sense that guides them well in doing so.

As a parent, I feel a spirituality should honor a child's humanness and the splendor of the physical world. The purpose of spirituality is not simply to provide a structure of meaning in which to live a life, but to tap an energy that embraces structures and enjoys them but can transcend them as well. It is not simply to give a child a set of beliefs, but a vision of the wonder and immensity of creation. It should open her heart to the grace and love that fills that immensity.

In the presence of such wonder and grace, spirituality should quicken a child's imagination. Of all the gifts and talents we have that make us human, the power to imagine is surely one of the greatest. Everything we have in our world that was created by a person, from paper clips to democracy, from televisions to farming, sprang from human imagination. Someone looked at the world and asked, "What if . . . ?" Someone had a vision of a possibility, a potential. If we wish to shape our futures, we do so first in imagination. In fact, if we want to see at all, we do so through imagination, which literally transforms the raw electromagnetic impulses that strike our optic nerve into images of houses and pets, parents and children, rainbows and forests, and all the other elements of our world.

All too often, out of familiarity and habit, we as adults and parents fail to grasp the power of this gift. We may denigrate the power and importance of imagination, thinking it fantasy and nonsense. We want our children to see the "real" world. But before we insist that our children see the world as we have seen it, we should listen to how they may see it with fresh eyes and an imaginative heart. After all, the paradigmatic scientist of our era, Albert Einstein, said that imagination was more important than knowledge, and he spoke from experience. It was his imaginative capacity rather than anything he could see in the "real" world that enabled him to look at the universe in a new way and develop his theories of relativity. He saw what no one else had seen because he had not blinded the eyes of his imagination.

It is imagination that allows me to touch the soul of another, to enter their heart and know them deeply. Compassion arises from imagination, which can leap over the boundaries of differences between us and find the common ground we share. Friendship and love emerge from it as surely as do stories and paintings and the fancies of our daydreams.

Spirituality arises from imagination as well. It is through my power to imagine—to go beyond material reason and logic—that I can encounter the sacred. It is in the realm of imagination that I find a pathway into the mystical. And it is there that God finds me. Indeed, I believe that the universe emerges from the play of God, filled with the delight and wonder of imagination. If past generations of mystics have called God the Great Architect, Mathematician, or Geometer of the universe, then, borrowing a wonderful term from Walt Disney, I would call God the Great Imagineer.

From a spiritual and practical standpoint, as mystic and parent, I want my children to be imagineers, too. I want them to see the world not only as it is but also as it could be. I want them to see the world that their eyes and ears cannot perceive but that unfolds in splendor from their hearts and their spirits—a world of love and delight, of connection and compassion, of fostering and potential. Then their minds and their spirituality will have room to expand, stretching their souls, in the immortal words of Buzz Lightyear, "to infinity . . . and Beyond!"

CALLING

THERE ARE AS MANY WAYS OF IMPLEMENTING OUR PAR-
enting and "mysting" as there are individual parents and mystics. Each family is different, each child is an individual, and
each mystic finds God and develops a relationship with the
sacred in a unique way.

God is not only in the details. God is in the differences.

On the other hand, however we parent or however we

myst, whatever vocation or passion may engage us in life, we all share one common calling. We are all co-creators of the future. We all have a responsibility for the shape that tomorrow will take. We exercise that responsibility through the decisions and choices we make, the visions we hold, and the quality of the lives that we build. Whether we act wisely and with intent or foolishly and blindly in our lives, whether we plan our steps or leap impulsively, we are always crafting the future. If our present is not all we had hoped it would be, then we must look to our responsibility in the matter and see what steps we can take to change it.

Like it or not, accept it or not, we all live on the future's edge, and our actions help shape what will emerge.

This calling to shape the future is especially significant for parents, for in our children, we work with the very fabric of our tomorrows. Parents create futures. That is the essence of what we do. As I help John-Michael, Aidan, Kaitlin, and Maryn discover their own unique voices, build their characters, develop values and visions, and gain skills, I am contributing to the world they will build. Perhaps one of them will become president of the United States or secretary-general of the United Nations. Perhaps one will win a Nobel Prize. Perhaps one will become a great writer who brings vision and insight to the world. Perhaps one will become a famous comedian, giving millions the gift of laughter.

Then again, perhaps not.

The wonderful thing is, they don't need to do any of these things to bless the future. Whatever they do, however humble, however grand, as long as it proceeds impeccably from the integrity of their own souls, it will be sufficient. As a parent, I am the one with the most immediate opportunities to empower them to do that.

In our Western culture, we are deeply influenced by the myth of the Hero, the lone individual whose great deeds turn the tide, transform the world, and save humanity. Stories of heroes and heroines are woven into the fabric of our lives from our earliest days. How can we not admire them and want to emulate them? Who would not want to perform great miracles and deeds of renown? Mystics are not immune to this heroic call, either. Who wouldn't want to call up vast spiritual forces, open new pathways to the sacred, heal the sick, part the sea, or raise the dead?

But more often than not, humanity is transformed by small deeds and small miracles that go unnoticed at the time. Who noticed two young guys named Steve and Joe working on a strange box in their garage back in the late seventies? Yet from their labor came the Apple, the first personal computer, and the founding of a whole new industry that in twenty years has changed the world as profoundly as anything since the printing press. Who knows what your teenagers are cooking up in your garage that will pioneer a similar leap forward?

Still, one does not have to invent new devices or create new industries to change the world or work miracles. The ability to raise a family—to see a single cell through nine months of intense development into a baby, and then see that baby through twenty years of challenge and opportunity to becoming a productive, loving, intelligent, imaginative, and creative human being—is truly a miracle. The effects may seem small compared to what a president or a pope might do, but this is the miracle on which the fate of our civilization rests. We all know the havoc that can be created by leaders whose parents were abusive, neglectful, or addicted. Think of Hitler. Do we want a president who had a toxic upbringing? Or what about the CEO of a multinational corporation, who wields more real power than most national leaders? Wouldn't the world be a safer, healthier, better place if our heads of state and captains of industry had all been raised by mothers and fathers who saw parenting as their primary calling, who brought to it the best of their intelligence, time, energy, and love? And wouldn't the world also be a better place if those leaders were all doing the same with their children?

So many children in the world today are being physically, emotionally, mentally, and spiritually abused in such a depressingly wide variety of ways. Creating a loving family in which a child can know safety, support, empowerment, and love is surely one of the most profound acts of service that any human being can provide. If at times the darkness of the world seems to press in close, then healthy, happy families—whatever shape or form they take, as long as the children within them are protected and enabled to grow in balanced ways—are part of the bulwark that protects us and part of the force that pushes back the darkness. If any mystic is looking for a calling, for a place to work meaningful miracles, then to be a good and sane parent is certainly worthy of the most careful consideration. If any parent wonders, in the midst of all the turmoil, sacrifice, struggle, and challenge of raising a family, if it is worth it, then he or she can reflect that there are reasons beyond mere metaphors of authority or power why the sacred is so often characterized as a father or a mother.

Parents have the opportunity to re-create daily the presence of the sacred in the very substance of what they do. They can ensure that through their lives and their efforts, and the lives and efforts of their children, Life itself will take a step forward and the world will be blessed because of it.

LOVE

IN THE FINAL ANALYSIS, BOTH PARENTING AND MYSTI-
cism come down to love. This is so basic and so often repeated
that it is a cliché. But—precisely because it is so fundamental—how can I write a book on either parenting or the mystical path without clearly reinforcing its importance?

The task of both the parent and the mystic is to open
channels through which love may more fully enter the world.
The mystic does this through the instruments of his or her

own heart and mind and body. The parent does this by offering the world new individuals in whom the light and blessing and power of love can find new forms of expression.

When I see my children having faith in themselves, listening to each other, fostering each other, and acting in compassionate ways, that is when I feel successful as a parent. If I see my children loving in ways that transcend my own—opening their hearts to the world in ways that I may have been unable to do—and if I can therefore learn from *them* more about being loving, then I have fulfilled my role both as parent and as mystic. How they embody that love, that presence of the Beloved, in their lives—whatever their professions, their vocations, their hobbies, or their callings—is up to them. Being able to embody it is the gift I wish to give them. It is the greatest inheritance of all, one that my parents and Julie's parents passed on to us in good measure, and one that defines our commitment to our children. It is the legacy that will help them define the culture in which they live and the future they will co-create.

Love is the place where the parent and mystic meet. It is the center, the attractor, that connects them and gives them meaning and power. You can have all the elements of a spiritual practice, and you can do all the things that a good parent is supposed to do, but if love is not there, you only have forms from which spirit is absent. You have bone and blood but no soul.

The bone and blood are important, too. When I think of love, I think of something robust and intelligent, vigorous and skillful, grounded and wise. It is not a vague feeling or a diffused emotion. It is embodied in action, in behavior, in relationship, and in responsibility. Love as a feeling is not enough; what we want is love as the full-bodied expression of a life lived compassionately and intelligently with a sense of its connectedness with a greater whole.

Love is spirit incarnate: powerful, courageous, and splendid. It is a light in the dark times, a spring in the dry times, a fire in the cold times, and a gathering of allies in the fearful and questioning times. It is not ignorant of consequences or uncaring of effects. It is passionate and disciplined, wild and domesticated, a demanding task and a delightful play. It is a paradox, a presence with many faces.

Love is also very simple and immediate: a snuggly hug, a lap, a warm washcloth on a teary face. It is the gift of time in a busy life, a word of advice, a word of praise, a listening ear, a prayerful heart, an unbreakable commitment.

Parents and mystics both come to know the many faces of love as they explore and serve the mystery of an emerging soul, on the one hand, or an emerging sacredness, on the other. When all is said and done, it is the same emergence in both instances.

And the same love that makes it so.

EDGES

SEATTLE IS THE CITY OF COFFEE AND CLOUDS, A PLACE where lattés live and the sun dies. But we have our golden days, too, when no cloud interrupts the blue statement of the sky, and the surrounding mountains stand against the horizon so clear and sharp that you could slice your eyes just looking at them.

On such a day I drive my son John-Michael to a local beach

to take his final qualifying dive for his scuba certification. This is a much-anticipated event for him. The dive has been postponed once already because of bad weather. His teacher explained that rain and pollen reduce the visibility under the water, and since we have an abundance of both in this area, I imagine that we have a lot of squinty-eyed fish in Puget Sound.

We are the first to arrive, and once we are parked, John-Michael begins unloading his gear with all the energy of an excited fourteen-year-old. This means that before I have un-limbered my fifty-two-year-old body from behind the steer-ing wheel, his oxygen tanks, dry suit, and various tubes, hoses, harnesses, and electronic gadgets are out of the car and stacked neatly on a retaining wall by the beach—a speed that would make a Seahawk receiver green with envy. This is a primo moment for him. He has worked hard all winter and spring as a paperboy in our neighborhood to earn the money to pay for his lessons and acquire his equipment.

As we wait for the rest of his class and his teacher to ar-rive, an ultralight flies over. A single-seat powered glider, not unlike a bicycle with wings, it looks to me like something built of hope and chutzpah masquerading as an airplane. But to John-Michael's eyes it is beautiful, a thing of grace and freedom. His life dream is to be a pilot like his uncle and grandfather, and he covets an ultralight the way kids in my generation coveted hot rods. He has informed me that there is no legal age restriction on flying one of these things. But for now, at least, his piloting is limited to computer flight simulations, which involve less wear and tear on both the family budget and my nerves.

Seeing the ultralight is a good omen for his dive. His love of flying is one reason he wanted to learn to scuba dive, for swimming underwater has the same feel of vertical and horizontal freedom. In his mind, if he can't fly a plane yet, then scuba diving is the next best thing.

Finally his instructor and the rest of his class arrive. The lengthy process of instruction, drill, devising a diving plan, suiting up, and checking each other's suits, fittings, gauges, and tubes begins—all of which will take a good thirty minutes or more. While this is going on, I wander over to a nearby espresso shop and treat myself to a mocha. The odd thing is that I don't really like coffee. But something about the clear, cool day, the excitement of the dive, and the fact that this is, after all, Seattle, the coffee-drinking capital of North America, conspire to weaken my resistance. And, I have to admit, the hot, steaming drink tastes good, in full harmony with the morning.

By the time I get back to the beach, everyone is suited up. Johnny looks like a spaceman in his bulky dry suit, which, unlike a traditional wet suit, has extra insulation and bulk to keep him warm in the cold waters of the Sound. The red and black hood that each diver wears is so tight it distorts his features, pushing his lips forward into a pout. He looks like some aboriginal native whose lips have been distended for ritual purposes.

Finally, the whole class, looking collectively like strange red and black creatures carrying large cylindrical eggs on their backs, waddles across the beach and enters the water. In the shallows they help each other to put on their flippers and check each other's equipment one last time. I am very gratified to see how serious everyone is about safety.

I sit on the retaining wall, sipping my mocha. Beside me is a book I intend to read while waiting for John-Michael to return. For the moment, though, I cannot take my eyes off the class. I watch them move further out into the water to a buoy that marks the place of their dive. Their plan is to go down some forty feet and spend half an hour exploring. By the time they reach the buoy, all I can see is a cluster of bobbing red and black heads. I cannot tell which one is my son. Then a figure turns and waves to me, and I wave back.

Abruptly, they are gone.

They have slipped beneath the waves so smoothly and suddenly that it is as if they were never there. I didn't even see them go under, and I am disturbed by that. I'm not sure what I expected: flippers upending, water splashing, trumpets from heaven. I don't know, but it seems unfair that they disappeared so quickly without some event marking their passage from one world to another.

Seeing how easily and completely my son can slip from my view, I begin to feel uneasy. I imagine dangers facing him underwater. I know it is irrational, I know the class will all be safe, I know what a fanatic their instructor is about safety and working together as buddies and as a team to look out for one another, and yet . . .

And yet, I am a father. My son has just gone into a world where I cannot follow, where I cannot see what is happening to him, where I cannot be there to protect him if danger should threaten. The undersea world is barred to me because of my chronic asthma; I cannot pass the physical that would permit me to dive with him. So he must go by himself into that other world, and I must stay behind.

On impulse, I stand up on the wall and peer out at the distant buoy, dipping and rising in the soft tumble of the waves. Julie, who accompanied John-Michael on his earlier dives, told me I could track his progress underwater by looking for air bubbles at the surface. I strain to see, but if such bubbles are rising up, I can't make them out.

Without warning, I am overwhelmed by a feeling of poignancy as bittersweet as the mocha in my hands. Searching the ocean for where John-Michael has disappeared, I suddenly find myself in the grip of an emotional undertow as powerful as any current he might be finding under the water.

I sit back down. Any thought of reading my book has vanished. I take a sip of the mocha, which is no longer hot and does not taste as good as it did, and make my own dive into this feeling that has so surprisingly and unexpectedly filled my heart. As I do, there arises in me an image of what it means to be a parent, an image that goes beyond the usual thoughts about child-raising and responsibility, loving and letting go. It is an image of an edge, like the beach I am on, which is a boundary between the sea and the land. It is an edge between the known and the unknown, the past and the future, the familiar and the mysterious, the traditional and the transformative, the existing and the emerging.

When I was a child, I was a scrambler. I loved to climb and clamber around on rocks and cliffs, and if there was an edge to look over, that was where I wanted to be. Of course, this caused my father no end of worry; I can still hear his voice in my mind: "Stay away from the edge!"

This is not bad advice. Some edges can cut you, and some you can fall over. Each of my four children is even more of a scrambler than I was. So I find myself, like my father before me, reminding my kids to be careful of knives and scissors, rooftops and cliffs, and other things that can be preludes to the emergency room.

Unfortunately, some edges cannot be avoided if we wish to open our kids' lives, and our own, to ongoing development. After all, our growth and unfoldment take place at edges where we encounter what we do not yet know, where we are open to learning and to change. Beyond these edges lies a world over which we have little control, and about which we can make few sure predictions—a world of possibilities where our only certain knowledge is that we will be transformed in some manner.

A parent is called to be a home-builder and a maintainer of a place of stability, nourishment, and safety. But a parent is also called to stand at the edge of that home and be a gateway to the world beyond the yard, beyond the picket fence, beyond the safety and the familiarity and the rituals of belonging and child-raising. Like me on my beach, a parent is asked to bring each child to the larger ocean of life, to walk him out to the edge of the dock. Then he must stand and watch as his child dives in, head bobbing for a while on the surface, and then suddenly disappears as she enters that larger world to find her own way—his own uniqueness—their own depths. This dichotomy between being the protector and creator of home and being the pathway into the unknown is the sharp edge at the heart of parenting.

It is the sense of being at this edge that bears down on me as I wait on the beach for the sea to give me back my son.

The mystic's path is no different. It takes me to a similar edge, the boundary between self and not-self, the finite and the infinite, the known and the Mystery. And the ocean of God has depths beyond those any earthly sea can match.

Yet once you plunge into that ocean, you discover a strange and loving thing, for far from disappearing, God gives you back to yourself in a new way. You can walk the earth and still know, like your blood knows the ancient ocean from which we all came, the depths of the love from which all things emerge.

Without warning, and closer to shore than I had anticipated, John-Michael appears, making his way, weary and exultant, toward the beach. He has returned from the sea, and for now he is back on my side of the edge. This dive is finished. But as I help him ashore, I know it is only a prelude to the greater ones that await us both.

SUGGESTED READING

There are many wonderful books on parenting and child-raising these days—many more than I can list. I would encourage any reader seeking advice on these topics to browse through his or her local bookstore or library and see what meets his or her needs.

Here are two resources that Julie and I have found invaluable:

The Parent's Handbook and *Parenting Young Children*, by Don Dinkmeyer, Sr., et al., American Guidance Services (1-800-328-2560). The key manuals of the Systematic Training for

Effective Parenting (STEP) program, which provides truly insightful and practical training for parents. Julie uses these textbooks in her parenting classes.

Your Two-Year-Old, Your Three-Year-Old, Your Four-Year-Old, etc., by Louise Bates Ames and Frances L. Ilg, Delacorte Press, 1976. A series of books on child-raising from the Gesell Institute of Child Development; each book focuses on the needs, strengths, challenges, and concerns of a particular age. We have found this series an invaluable aid in understanding our children and improving our parenting skills.

Here is a short list of books on parenting that we have enjoyed:

Caring for the Family Soul, by Amy E. Dean, Berkley, 1996.

Everyday Blessings: The Inner Work of Mindful Parenting, by Myla and Jon Kabat-Zinn, Hyperion, 1997.

The Mother Dance, by Harriet Lerner, HarperCollins, 1998.

Our Share of Night, Our Share of Morning: Parenting as a Spiritual Journey, by Nancy Fuchs, HarperCollins, 1996.

Raising Children in a Material World: Introducing Spirituality into Family Life, by Phil Catalfo, Berkley, 1997.

The Shelter of Each Other: Rebuilding Our Families, by Mary Pipher, Grosset/Putnam, 1996.

The following books are not specifically about parenting or child-raising, but they provide excellent insights into the challenges facing adolescents. As a parent preparing for those challenges, I certainly benefited from reading them:

The Dance of the Dissident Daughter, by Sue Monk Kidd, Harper-Collins, 1996.

Letters to My Son: Reflections on Becoming a Man, by Kent Nerburn, New World Library, 1994.

Reviving Ophelia, by Mary Pipher, Ballantine, 1994.

Finally, if you enjoyed this book, you might like reading my earlier ones on spirituality and the transformation of culture:

A Pilgrim in Aquarius, Findhorn Press, 1996. About my own encounter with the New Age/Transformational movements and my personal perspective on their underlying spiritual ideas.

Everyday Miracles, Bantam, 1996. Personal creativity, manifestation, and tapping the power of synchronicity and flow in one's life.

Reimagination of the World: A Critique of the New Age, Science, and Popular Culture, co-authored with William Irwin Thompson, Bear, 1991. As the title says, a critical yet sympathetic look at the historical and spiritual dimensions of the idea of cultural transformation and the birth of a New Age.

The Call, Riverhead Books, 1996. Explores the deeper aspects of one's general calling in life, as well as the idea of a spiritual vocation.

David **Spangler** is the author of *Revelation: The Birth of a New Age*, *Emergence: The Rebirth of the Sacred*, *Everyday Miracles*, *A Pilgrim in Aquarius*, and most recently *The Call*. He also coauthored *Reimagination of the World* with William Irwin Thompson. In addition to writing, David lectures and teaches workshops and long-term classes. He lives in Seattle with his wife, Julie, and their four children.